The
Investor's Guide to
Measuring Share
Performance

The
Investor's Guide to
Measuring Share
Performance

DAN MACFIE

PITMAN PUBLISHING
128 Long Acre, London WC2E 9AN

A Division of Pearson Professional Limited

First published in Great Britain 1994

British Library Cataloguing in Publication Data
A CIP catalogue record for this book can be obtained from the British Library.

ISBN 0 273 60628 X

No responsibility for loss occasioned to any person acting or refraining from
action as a result of the material in this publication can be accepted by the
author or publishers. If in doubt always seek professional investment advice.

10 9 8 7 6 5 4

Phototypeset in Linotron Times Roman
by Northern Phototypesetting Co. Ltd., Bolton
Printed and bound in Great Britain
by Biddles Ltd, Guildford and King's Lynn

The Publishers' policy is to use paper manufactured from sustainable forests

CONTENTS

13 SUMMARY OF THE SYSTEM

APPENDICES

FOREWORD

The Investor's Guide to Measuring Share Performance is a useful addition to the large number of books written for the private investor in that it tackles this important issue from a practical viewpoint. Most books in this field describe how to invest and review the merits of the different types of investment, whereas Dan Macfie's book concentrates on how to measure the performance of an individual share and a portfolio of shares.

There are a large number of computer literate private investors, with relatively small portfolios, who at present do not have the means to measure performance, but for whom a quantified assessment is important. This book is ideally suited to meet their needs.

A range of methods of measurement are described in the book, with a limited number recommended for use by the private investor. The principles behind the different methods are detailed, making it easier for the readers to choose or develop a system of performance analysis that is tailor-made to their own particular requirements. Ease of calculation has been an important consideration in Dan Macfie's choice of methods. This pragmatic approach has succeeded with little loss of accuracy, although any potential loss of accuracy has been studiously documented.

I believe that all investors should measure the performance of their shares and portfolio. If you are a private investor, whether with a small or large portfolio, and you want to do it yourself, this is the book for you.

Gordon Bagot, Director of Research and Consultancy,
The WM Company
Crewe Toll
EDINBURGH
December 1993

PREFACE

When I retired from full time work in August 1988, I decided that I should take a more active interest in investments. I already had a few shares and unit trusts, and there was also a small lump sum waiting to be invested. Over the years I had occasionally jotted down the share and unit trust prices, but had no idea of how to analyse the performance of the investments. I did begin to record the FT 30 share index and had toyed with the idea of calculating the ratio of the share price to the index – the only guidance I had found in reading books on investment. A more thorough search of the books on the subject in the library and the bookshops brought no further help.

It was at this stage that I bought my computer, with the vague intention of developing a system of performance analysis. I also thought it would be interesting to learn how to use a computer; the nearest I had come to this previously had been at management courses, including three days at IBM. I had for many years, of course, been using the output of computers operated by my younger colleagues.

My background in science and engineering and my experience of management in industry convinced me that satisfactory progress depended to a large extent on the measurement of performance and the establishment of targets or budgets. Those who work in industry, at all levels, are regularly monitoring critical criteria calculated from measurements of dimensions, weights, value, etc. A knowledge of the fuel used by a chemical plant, for instance, does not tell you how efficiently it is being operated. By calculating the fuel used per tonne of output, however, the performance of the plant can be monitored, and efficiency improvements will follow. The regular calculation and monitoring of the return on investment is a requirement of factory management and the board of directors of every company of any size. Applying the same principles to the management of a portfolio of investments, it was obvious that the recording of the price of a share was no substitute for a thorough system of performance measurement. The record of the price, together other pieces of information, such as the All Share Index and the Retail Price Index, needed to be converted into meaningful performance criteria, to allow private investors to control their investments and improve their performance. I was convinced that investors were not implementing these principles because they did not have available for use an easily understood system of performance measurement. Having reached this conclusion it seemed obvious that I should write up my System of performance measurement in a form suitable for publication.

By early 1992, having written down my preliminary ideas, I asked some of my former colleagues at British Alcan Aluminium to pass comment. Since then they have given me invaluable help and support, particularly Tom Dougan and Barry Purnell at Alcan Chemicals.

By June 1993 I had completed the foundations of the System of share performance measurement for private investors, and approached the WM Company in Edinburgh, a world leader in the measurement of investment performance. Robert Darling read the book and was supportive and constructive in his comments. I then met Gordon Bagot, the Director of Research and Consultancy, who wrote the Foreword, for which I am most grateful.

Finally I should like to record my sincere thanks to my family for their tolerance and support and particularly to my sons, Andrew and Alistair, for their help, and above all to my wife, Mildred, for maintaining her natural good nature whilst I spent so much time 'playing with my computer'.

Dan Macfie
January, 1994

1

INTRODUCTION

'Money speaks sense in a language all nations understand.'
Aphra Behn, 1640–1689

GENERAL

Many people nowadays have invested part of their savings in shares, either directly in ordinary shares or through unit trusts, investment trusts or personal equity plans (Peps). The number of investors is increasing and will continue to increase in the future. Furthermore, many of these investors are accustomed to monitoring performance at work, often with the help of a computer. In ever greater numbers, therefore, investors will want to have a system which will allow them to monitor the performance of their shares.

In investing, as in business, investors or managers will study their subject before taking part in the action. The most important stage in any learning process, however, is in the taking part, and in order to learn the most from experience a means for assessing performance is a necessity. The purpose of this book is to provide private investors with a system for monitoring the performance of their shares which is flexible enough to meet the needs of both the first-time investor and the person who has already accumulated a portfolio of shares. This will be designated *The System* and is designed to be straightforward to use, to absorb little time, and to express the performance of the shares in quantitative, rather than qualitative, terms. Many financial commentators talk of shares having performed well or badly, without defining the criteria for their judgement. Often seen in newspapers are comments that, for instance, a particular share had done well, its price having doubled in the last X years. No mention is made of the fact that the Retail Price Index (RPI), over the same period, had more than doubled, or that the All Share Index (AlShI) had tripled. In fact, therefore, the share had not performed well, having lost value in real terms, whilst the average share had increased its real value by 50 per cent. If it is true that the reading public gets the quality of financial comment that it deserves, then helping investors by pro-viding them with a system for measuring the performance of their shares should significantly improve the quality of reporting and com-ment in the press and magazines. The emphasis, therefore, is to define clearly the criteria used in assessing performance and to express the performance in figures rather than in subjective terms. Only those methods which are elegant, concise and easily understood have been included in the System.

There are a number of subjects in the field of investing that are deliberately not discussed in this book, since they have been very adequately covered in many other publications. There is no discus-sion of the way the stock market works, how to buy or sell shares, the relative advantages and disadvantages of different types of invest-ment or the interpretation of company accounts. It has been assumed that readers have already informed themselves on these subjects. The one subject, however , which is not adequately dealt with in the books and magazines read by the private investor, is the measurement of the performance of each of the individual shares in a portfolio, and of the portfolio itself. This is possibly a consequence of the fact that a computer is needed to do the job easily for even a small portfolio of shares, and that until recently computers of the required power were too expensive for the private investor to buy. Furthermore, it is only recently that a significant proportion of the investing public has acquired the confidence and the moderate skills necessary to use a computer for this purpose.

Use of the System described in this book does not require any great mathematical ability. The System is written in a form that is useable whether or not a computer and spreadsheet software are available to the reader. Once the number of different shares held increases to more than a handful, however, the assessment of performance becomes laborious without the use of a computer. When the reader does have a computer it is sensible, in addition to using it to measure performance, to store on the computer the data relating to all the shares held, such as date purchased, purchase price and certificate identification number(s). The System also produces the information needed for income tax and capital gains tax purposes.

The only options available to private investors at the present time are to design their own system for measuring the performance of their shares, or to invest in the purchase of software for this purpose . The advantage of being able to design a system tailor-made for their own particular requirements is generally negated by the lack of expertise of the investor in designing software for investment purposes; this is also a very time-consuming process. To buy the correct software is also difficult because investors often only have a vague notion of what they require at this stage and buying the wrong software can be very expensive. This book has been written to provide the private investor with the solution to this dilemma. For the cost involved in buying this book investors can obtain a system for the measurement of invest-ment performance that can be put into immediate use, either manually or on their computer. The chosen method of approach in each section is explained, together with the reasons for rejecting other alternatives. The system proposed is flexible and can be easily adapted by investors to suit their own requirements or preferences.

Provided with the book, on purchase, is a computer floppy disk containing the tables of market statistics and the data and perform-ance calculations for a selected portfolio of shares. This disk helps the reader in two important ways:

(a) those readers, whose first priority is to put the System into use can simply replace the share names, numbers and prices on the disk with the same data for the shares in their own portfolio. Alternatively, they can add their own companies to the list already on the disk. The necessary equations are also stored on the disk, so that the performance data will be produced with the minimum of time and effort.

(b) for those readers who have the time to study the principles behind the System, this is made easier by reading the data from the floppy disk on the computer screen simultaneously with the book. The way in which the equations have been used is also easier to understand, since, when the contents of a cell have been calculated by means of an equation, the equation is displayed when the cell pointer is moved to the cell.

A situation not so far considered is the one where investors employ some organisation, such as a bank, to manage their portfolios. This book could be valuable to such investors, because the system expresses performance in a way that is better than many of the conventional methods. It is suggested that owners of managed portfolios should request regular reports on the *real growth*, yield and *real return* of their portfolios, together with the corresponding targets. Such investors will only need to read parts of the book to understand the value of such reports.

STRUCTURE OF THE BOOK AND THE COMPUTER PROGRAM

This chapter has given a very brief outline of the reasons for writing this book. The next two chapters (2 and 3) discuss the advantages to be gained from measuring share performance, and the criteria used in the measurement. A chapter (4) is then devoted to an example of the performance criteria produced by the System, for an individual share (ICI) and for a *selected portfolio* of shares. The intention of this section is to allow the reader to obtain a clear understanding of the objectives, before working through the explanations and examples which follow.

Chapter 5 outlines the methods adopted for measuring the performance of individual shares, whilst Chapter 6 does the same for portfolios. The special case of Peps is dealt with in Chapter 7. Examples are given to help the reader understand each new concept as it is introduced into the System.

Two chapters (8 and 9) follow, in which the characteristics of the computer, the software and the files are discussed in relation to the size of the portfolio whose performance is to be measured. Chapter 9 also discusses the frequency with which data should be entered and the performance criteria calculated. For the performance of a share or a portfolio to be fully understood, it must be set in the context of the performance of the market as a whole. The information needed to do this is collected together in Chapter 10 and Table 13.1, which is also available on the floppy disk. Table 13.1 in the printed form has an end date for data recording and performance assessment of 30 December 1992, whilst the end date for the information on the floppy disk is 31 December 1993.

The System of performance measurement is then applied to a selected portfolio of shares, chosen to demonstrate particular facets of the System. The data and calculations are recorded in Tables 13.2 to 13.4 and on the floppy disk, and the results are summarised and discussed in Chapter 11. The end date of the review period in these Tables is 30 December 1992, whilst the end date for the performance data on the floppy disk is 31 December 1993. This chapter also gives advice on how to transfer the ownership of shares, for instance from a husband to his wife, without incurring costs. Fixed interest investments are the subject dealt with in Chapter 12 and the System is summarised in the final Chapter (13).

The printed version of Table 13.1, because of its size, is at the last Chapter (13). The three Tables, 13.2 to 13.4, which are much the largest in the book, follow Table 13.1. All the other tables and figures immediately follow the relevant comment in the text.

Appendix 1 contains a summary of the actions needed to put the System into use for the reader's own shares. For those investors with the time and interest to consider modifying the System to suit their own requirements, further information is given in Appendices 2, 3 and 4 on the principles behind the methods used, proofs of the formulae, and the accuracy of the calculation methods.

Finally, Appendices 5 and 6 review the alternative methods that were considered, but not chosen, for inclusion in the System.

Definitions of the terms used which have special significance are included in a Glossary, which follows the Appendices. Terms, such as *target growth*, which have a specific meaning in this book, are printed in italic type in the text, and are always included in the terms defined in the Glossary. Where abbreviations are used, these are also in the Glossary. The headings in the tables and the equations make use of abbreviations, rather than algebraic symbols; for instance, Infl and

AlShI represent per cent inflation/annum and the FT All Share Index respectively. This is intended to make the reading of the book easier for those readers unaccustomed to mathematical or scientific literature. The equations which are included are all simple and easily understood by the layman.

The floppy disk which is sold with the book contains:

Table 13.1 Market statistics

This table contains data on the performance of equity investments, starting with the three most commonly used share price indices. Performance criteria, such as the per cent real return per annum of the shares that go to make up the All Share Index, are calculated. The performance of a bank savings account is also calculated.

Tables 13.2, 13.3 and 13.4 Selected portfolio

These tables contain information about the shares in the *selected portfolio* and the calculations of the performance criteria.

The disk serves two purposes, firstly as an aid to reading and understanding the book, and secondly as a spreadsheet program into which data on the reader's own shares can be entered and the performance criteria calculated, using the equations already in the program. The original disk should be kept unaltered, copies being made for entering the reader's own share data, etc.

Performance measurements are carried out in Tables 13.1 to 13.4 over a range of periods. The performance measurements on the floppy disk end on 31 December 1993.

The first file on the disk, MspDisk, contains a description of the contents of the Tables 13.1 to 13.4.

2

WHY MEASURE SHARE PERFORMANCE?

'You pays your money and you takes your choice.'
Punch, 1846.

The measurement of share performance is essential to any investor for four reasons which are described below.

A share's past performance gives an indication, but no guarantee, of course, of future performance. The reason for this is not only that a company that has been well-managed in the past is likely to be well managed in the future; it is also because the share price and yield at any one time are measures of how investors value the company over the coming years. It can be argued that, in a perfect market, the share price is determined solely by investors' expectations of the future profitability of the company, and that past performance is irrelevant. It is, however, only necessary to read the financial press to see the importance that journalists and their readers put on a knowledge of past performance. Indeed many systems of share selection depend on past performance, the prime example being charting. In a book published recently and reviewed in April, 1993, with the title *How to Choose Stock Market Winners: a Minimum-Risk System for the Private Investor*, Raymond Caley recommends three criteria in choosing shares, two of which relate to past performance, as measured by the share price and the price-earnings ratio. Jim Slater in *The Zulu Principle*, published in 1992, uses the movement of the 'relative strength' of the share price as one of the criteria for selecting shares to purchase. It is generally accepted, therefore, that the record of a share's price, P/E ratio and yield is essential information for an investor to possess before buying or selling shares (including unit and investment trusts). The prime feature of the System recommended in this book is the way in which this information is handled in order to make it more meaningful. Standards have also been established, as part of the System, to provide a basis for comparison for the performance figures.

Investors use different methods for choosing shares to buy or sell. Fundamental analysis and charting are examples; another is to follow the recommendations of a financial journalist, stockbroker, or financial advisor. Whichever method has been used in the past, it should only continue to be used if it has proved to be successful and this can only be determined by measuring the performance of the individual shares and the portfolio.

Many people can expect to receive a lump sum at some time in the future, either as an inheritance or at the time of retirement. Such people could, with advantage, before receiving the lump sum, experiment with a number of methods for choosing shares for purchase and then monitor the performance of these shares over a period of years, without actually purchasing the shares. The individual would then be far better prepared to become an investor when the lump sum materialises.

The performance of fixed interest investments should be monitored on a regular basis. History indicates that there can be extended periods of time when bank deposit or building society savings accounts have performed better than equities. 1990 is a recent example; indeed this is the case for periods of a few years in the late 1980s and early 1990s, depending on the particular dates on which the review period starts and ends. Monitoring the relative performance of equities and fixed-interest investments can help investors choose the appropriate time to change the balance in their portfolio between these two types of investment.

3

WHAT TO MEASURE

'Let us be happy and live within our means, even if we have to borrer the money to do it with.'
Artemus Ward (Charles Farrer Brown), 1834–1867.

REASONS FOR SHARE PRICE CHANGES

Analysts use two basic pieces of data as measurements of the performance of a share. The first is the price at which the share can be bought or sold in the stock market and the pattern of change of the price over the past days, weeks, months and years. The second piece of data used to assess the performance of a share is the dividend paid to the owner. The latter is best expressed in terms of either the gross dividend yield or the net dividend yield (after deduction of standard rate tax). Any other data or information is only useful in helping to understand and predict the price and dividend performance of the shares. The comments of financial journalists and the figures for price/earnings ratio are available in the papers and magazines, and these assist in understanding the performance. Company annual reports are an important source of information, but cannot be relied upon to give accurate guidance on future prospects.

Changes in the share price, in particular, require a system of analysis to make them meaningful. The price of a share can go up or down for two separate reasons, one related to the economy as a whole, and the other unrelated to the economy, but dependent on factors unique to the company issuing the shares. It is important to know the relative importance of each of these possible reasons.

The System outlined in this book has been developed to answer this question, among others, and also to allow the performance of portfolios of shares to be assessed. (A more sophisticated assessment of performance would review the performance of the sector within which the company operated, e.g. banking, engineering, etc.).

COMPARISON WITH THE RETAIL PRICE INDEX AND THE ALL SHARE INDEX

The System makes use of two basic concepts. Firstly, the performance of an individual share, or of a portfolio of shares, is assessed by monitoring the change, over a period of time, in the real value of the share or the portfolio. This gives an indication of whether the investments have retained their real value or purchasing power, i.e. their value after allowing for inflation, as measured by the Retail Price Index (RPI). Secondly, the change in the share price can be compared with the change in the FT All Share Index (AlShI), thereby assessing whether the share has changed in value by more or less than the average share. The implementation of these concepts can be achieved simply by monitoring the ratios of the price, firstly to the Retail Price Index and secondly to the All Share Index. A better option, although more complicated in calculation terms, is to calculate the real growth rate (per cent *real growth* per annum) in the share price. This is then compared with a target growth rate (per cent target growth/a.), which is the real growth rate the share(s) would have attained if its value had tracked the All Share Index. This would have been more correctly termed the per cent target real growth/a., but the briefer version was chosen as it takes less space in the headings in the spreadsheet.

A simple example helps to demonstrate why both indices are needed: a share which increases its value in real terms by 20 per cent per annum in two years is performing well, despite the fact that its value increases by 10 per cent per annum less than the All Share Index. On the other hand, a share which increases its value by 10 per cent per annum more than the All Share Index but loses 20 per cent per annum of its real value is obviously performing well compared with the average share, but is a poor investment. The yield must also

be monitored, of course, to allow a full assessment of share performance to be achieved. The yield of the shares in the All Share Index is
termed the *target yield*, and provides a basis of comparison for the
yields of individual shares and portfolios. These examples demonstrate the two requirements for success: choosing the right shares to
buy and getting the timing of the purchases and sales right. This is
certainly not as easy as it sounds, as demonstrated by the fact that
many unit trusts and investment trusts do not perform as well as the
All Share Index, despite the knowledge and experience of their
investment managers.

RETURN ON INVESTMENT

The growth rate of the share price and the yield are interrelated
variables. It is almost invariably found that a share whose price is
increasing more rapidly than the All Share Index, over a period of
years, has a lower yield than the average. Investors accept lower
dividends in the expectation of greater capital growth. To express the
same concept in a different way, investors are willing to pay a higher
price for a share, thereby bringing the yield below target, because
they expect the price and dividend growth in future to be above
target. An easy way to express the performance of a share by means
of a single variable is to calculate the total net real return on investment. This can be achieved easily and with sufficient accuracy for
most purposes by adding together the real growth rate and the
average net yield to give the real net return. For instance, a share
whose price is increasing in real terms by 7 per cent per annum and
having a net yield of 3 per cent, has a real net return of 10 per cent per
annum. Another share might have a real price growth of 3 per cent
per annum and a net yield of 7 per cent per annum, also resulting in a
real return of 10 per cent per annum. In the case of a share whose net
income is reinvested, with the effect of increasing the value of the
shares (accumulation units in a unit trust, for instance) the real net
return (called in future the *real return*) is equal to the *real growth*,
since the yield is nil. The *target return* is defined as the sum of the
target growth and the *target yield* (net), and is a measure of the

performance of the shares in the All Share Index.

To summarise, shares with a *real growth* greater than the *target growth*, over a period of years, will normally have a yield that is lower than the *target yield*, and vice versa. There will therefore be much less variation in the *real return* of shares than in the *real growth*.

Every effort has been made to ensure that the System is easy to understand and use, but where a choice has had to be made between simplicity and validity, the latter has been given priority with one exception, i.e. the calculation of the *real return* (see Chapter 5) over a period of years, where a simplified method has been adopted at the sacrifice of some accuracy. To recognise this the *real return* is always rounded off to an integer.

GENERAL

The conventional criteria for measuring investment performance in commerce and industry have not normally been corrected for the effect of inflation. Some investors will want to be able to measure share and portfolio performance by means of the conventional criteria, i.e. the rate of growth of the price (or portfolio value) and/or the rate of return on the investment in the share or the portfolio. They should only use these conventional criteria, rather than the *real growth* and *real return*, on special occasions; for instance, they might want to compare some current performance figures with past figures, which were expressed in traditional terms. This book gives the information needed for the investor to calculate the conventional criteria, since the calculation of both the *real growth* and the *real return* requires the calculation of the growth and the return first. Establishing standards of performance by calculating appropriate targets can, of course, be used equally well with the conventional criteria.

The System outlined in this book is mainly concerned with methods for measuring share and portfolio performance and with how to use this information to improve future investment performance. There is, however, one facet of the latter objective which is somewhat controversial, i.e. should a change in the price of a share, relative to the All Share Index, lead an investor to buy or sell the shares. The perfect market theory would indicate that even though the share price has fallen by 20 per cent, for instance, over the last few days, whilst the All Share Index has remained constant, the price nevertheless measures the current worth or value of the share in the light of all the available information. There is, therefore, no more reason to sell the share now than there was a few days ago. On the other hand it can be argued that all investors do not possess all the relevant information, either because some of it is not generally available or because some shareholders have missed its publication. A recent example was provided by Jeff Randall in the *Sunday Times* on 2 May 1993, who wrote:

> 'Inspired selling of Tiphook shares was rewarded on Thursday when the container and trailer-leasing group issued a shock profits warning. Having been 380p on April 1, Tiphook's shares opened last week at 329p. The price dropped 4.2 per cent on Monday to 315p, and a further 6.9 per cent on Tuesday to 293p. Red lights began flashing, but for most investors it was too late. After the announcement that Tiphook's profits would be about 20 per cent below market forecasts, the stock went into freefall, crashing to 170p before bouncing back to 232p after some directors' buying. The fall wiped £100m off the company's market worth. The stock exchange is investigating the share-price slump. It could, of course, be a coincidence: a few punters getting lucky. But I doubt it. Someone, somewhere, knew something – and traded.'

Examples such as this lead to the conclusion that the market for shares cannot be regarded as a 'perfect market'. It is a fact that many investors do regard a falling share price as a trigger to sell, and vice versa. Readers are left to make their own judgement on this matter. Monitoring of the movement in the price of a share, relative to the All Share Index, is believed to be worthwhile, if only to warn investors that they should ensure that they are aware of the reason for the movement.

STANDARDS OF COMPARISON

The *target return* of equities is largely determined by the *real return* investors can get from fixed interest investments such as gilts, plus an allowance which investors' judge necessary to compensate for the risks of equity investment. The yield ratio, the ratio of the yield on equities to the yield on long-dated gilts, has been been in the range 2 to 2.5 over most of the last 10 years. One suitable standard of comparison for an investor's shares is provided by index-linked gilts. These government stocks, in addition to retaining their real value, have shown a net yield of 3 per cent to 4 per cent per annum to redemption; i.e. their *real return* is 3 to 4 per cent per annum. Most index-linked gilts have been issued with a coupon of 2.5 per cent, so that if they are purchased on issue and held to redemption, the *real return* will be near to 2 per cent per annum (the exact figure depends on the basic rate of tax). Since there is no risk in investing in index-linked gilts if they are held to redemption, their performance can be regarded as a minimum target at which an investor should aim. Another standard of performance is provided by a bank or building society savings account, and the three-month inter-bank interest rate has been taken to represent such investments; their *real return* over the period 31 March 1982 to 30 December 1992 has been 3 per cent per annum.

Because of the risk, equity investments must perform better than the fixed interest accounts detailed in the last paragraph over the longer term, and indeed this has been so, but the average growth actually achieved depends upon the period over which the growths are measured. Over the more than 10 years from 31 March 1982 to 30 December 1992, the All Share Index has grown by almost four times, from 323 to 1358, whilst the Retail Price Index has increased by less than twice, from 80 to 140 (see Chapter 10). The average share, as represented by the All Share Index, has, therefore, more than doubled its value in real terms. (The word average is used in a general, rather than a mathematical sense. The All Share Index is a weighted average, the weighting taking account of the capitalisation of each company). As will be shown in Chapter 5 this is equivalent to a *real growth* of 8.6 per cent per annum, and is called the *target growth*. The yield of the shares in the All Share Index has been in the range 4 to 6 per cent (say 3.5 per cent net); this is called the *target yield*. The average *real return*, i.e. the *target return* has therefore been about 12 per cent per annum over the 10 plus years. The *target growth, target yield* and *target return* are measures of the performance of the All Share Index, i.e. the average share, in real terms, and are therefore suitable standards against which the *real growth*, yield and *real return* of a share or a portfolio can be compared. The detailed figures for these variables, covering various periods since 31 March 1982, are recorded in Table 13.1.

To assist the discussion, five different levels of performance of equity investments are defined and summarised below. The performance levels apply equally to individual shares or to portfolios.

Performance levels

Minimum:	matches the *real return* of an index-linked gilt.
Moderate:	achieves a *real return* of 7 per cent per annum but falls short of the *target return*.
Satisfactory:	matches the *target return* and achieves a *real return* of 7 per cent.
Good:	achieves a *real return* of 12 per cent per annum.
Excellent:	shows at least a *real return* of 17 per cent per annum.

SUMMARY

To summarise, a System of performance measurement is needed to provide an investor with the information to:

(a) Assist in deciding when to buy and sell, and which shares to buy and sell.
(b) Check whether satisfactory results are being produced by the investment method/system/advice used by the investor.
(c) Compare one type or category of investment with another; e.g. ordinary shares, unit trusts, investment trusts, (these three being referred to as shares in this book), Peps, gilts, bank and building society savings accounts, etc.

To satisfy these needs, the following requirements for the System, designed primarily to measure the performance of an equity investment over a period of time, have been chosen.

The System must:

(1) Be capable of being applied to either one particular share or a portfolio of shares.

(2) Measure the real growth and real return in the value of the investment, i.e. the growth and the return after taking into account the loss in value of the £ sterling due to inflation, using the change in the Retail Price Index as the measure of inflation.

(3) Compare the performance of a share or portfolio with the same investment in the FT All Share Index.

(4) Provide other criteria for comparison with equity performance, e.g. real return on gilts and bank savings.

(5) Be easy to understand and simple to use, whilst providing the minimum data required to assess the performance of the investment.

(6) Monitor the performance of the investments over both the long-term and the short-term.

(7) Produce the pattern of change of the criteria used to monitor performance, over the period of the review, and not just the average of each of the criteria.

(8) Produce the data needed for the calculation of income tax and capital gains tax.

(9) Be flexible enough to allow investors to modify it to suit their own requirements.

When terms such as value, gain, growth and return are used, preceded by the word real, it means that the value, etc., have been corrected for the effect of inflation, using the Retail Price Index as the index.

Some of the other methods of performance assessment that were considered are described in the Appendices, and the reasons for not choosing them for inclusion in the System are outlined.

4

AN EXAMPLE OF PERFORMANCE MEASUREMENT

'Nobody was ever meant
To remember or invent
What he did with every cent.'
Robert Frost, 1874–1963

Two brief examples follow of the application of the System, the first to the assessment of the performance of an individual share and the second to a portfolio of shares. The information is extracted from the more detailed analysis described later in the book. The data for ICI shares are used in the first example, the holding being assumed to comprise 900 shares (note the difference between this number, chosen to highlight the benefit of the *real gain* calculation, and the number held in the *selected portfolio*); a portfolio of 12 different shares, called the *selected portfolio*, is used in the second example. The end date of the review period has been chosen as 30 December 1992 for the statistics and calculations used in this chapter, so that the results can be compared with those of all the other shares in the printed tables, 13.3 and 13.4. Another reason for the choice of this end date was that the data for the ICI shares was complicated in 1993 by the demerger of ICI into two companies: ICI and Zeneca. Inclusion of the data for 1993 at this stage would have negated the prime purpose of this chapter, which was to introduce the System of performance measurement to the reader. The finer points of the System will be dealt with later.

DATA FOR ICI SHARES

The ICI share prices and the indices, over a 10 year period, are shown in the graph in Figure 4.1. It is seen that the graph is of limited use and gives only a rough appreciation of the share performance over the years. The figures for the price/share, *RPI, AlShI, P/A ratio* and *real gain*, are listed in the first part of Table 4.1, followed in the second part, by the yield, *real growth* and *real return* and the corresponding *targets*. These figures allow a quantified assessment of performance, which is much more informative than the presentation in Figure 4.1. The explanation of these terms is given in the following paragraphs, whilst precise definitions and methods of calculation will be found when the reader reaches Chapter 5.

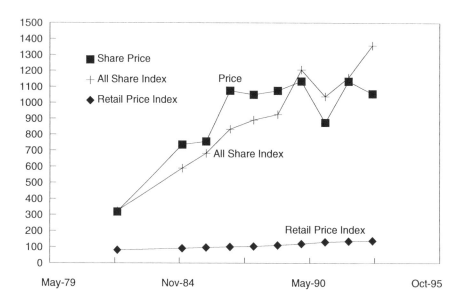

Figure 4.1   ICI shares: share prices and indices

Table 4.1 ICI; share price and performance

	Price p./share	RPI	AlShI	P/A ratio	Real gain £
31/03/82	318	80.2	323	1.17	
29/12/84	736	91.0	590	1.48	3370
31/12/85	756	96.1	682	1.32	3370
31/12/86	1075	99.8	833	1.53	6110
29/12/87	1075	103.3	891	1.43	5990
30/12/88	1050	110.6	926	1.35	5500
29/12/89	1134	119.1	1205	1.12	5950
28/12/90	874	130.1	1038	1.00	3220
27/12/91	1133	135.7	1157	1.16	5350
30/12/92	1056	138.6	1358	0.92	4560

	Gross Yield	Target Yield	% Growth/a. to 30/12/92		% Return/a. to 30/12/92	
	%	%	Real	Target	Real	Target
31/03/82		5.8	6.3	8.6	11	12
29/12/84	4.7	4.4	−0.7	5.3	4	9
31/12/85	5.7	4.3	−0.5	4.7	4	8
31/12/86	4.3	4.1	−5.6	2.7	−1	6
29/12/87	5.7	4.2	−6.0	2.6	−1	6
30/12/88			−5.3	4.0	0	8
29/12/89	5.9	4.2	−7.1	−1.1	−2	3
28/12/90	8.4	5.4	6.5	10.7	11	14
27/12/91	6.5	5.2	−8.7	14.7	−3	18
30/12/92	6.9	4.4				

PERFORMANCE OF ICI SHARES

One method of assessing the performance of a share is to monitor the variation in the *P/A ratio*. This is defined as the ratio 'Price/AlShI', rebased to 1.0 on 28 December 1990, and is used primarily for the short-term monitoring of the share price, in order to assist in buying and selling decisions. From Table 4.1 it is seen that the *P/A ratio* increased rapidly in the first few years of the review, responding to the higher turnover and expanding economy that followed the 1980 recession, as is normal for the chemical sector. Much of this increase was lost however, particularly when the economy began to slow down in 1989/90, and was only partly recovered when, in 1991, Hanson bought 2.8 per cent of the issued shares, leading the market to believe that a takeover bid was on the way. As the prospect of a take-over faded in late 1991 the price started to fall again, but this in turn was followed by a recovery in 1992 and then another serious fall, as can be seen from the trend in the *P/A ratio* over the 1991/92 period.

Trend in *P/A ratio*, quarterly from 28 December 1990 to 30 December 1992 : 1.00, 1.02, 1.27, 1.23, 1.16, 1.28, 1.19, 1.17, 0.92.

The *real gain* is the increase in the value of the holding of 900 shares, after allowing for inflation, since 31 March 1982. The figure obtained by subtracting the exemption limit (£5,800 in 1992/93 and 1993/94) from the *real gain* is the amount on which capital gains tax will have to be paid (after minor corrections for costs, etc.), if the holding is sold. The *real gain* is, therefore, a figure that is useful to have on a routine basis, so that it is easily available whenever the sale of the holding is being considered. The *real gain, P/A ratio*, yield and P/E ratio are therefore the criteria used to monitor the short-term performance of shares. The longer term performance makes use of the *real growth* and the *real return*.

The *real growth* for the ICI shares (see Table 4.1 and Figure 4.2) is the annual rate of growth in the price of the shares, after taking inflation into account, between the date recorded opposite the figure and the end of the review period, i.e. 30 December 1992. The *target growth* is the *real growth* that would have been achieved if the price of the share had tracked the All Share Index.

From Table 4.1 and Figure 4.2 it can be seen that the *real growth* in the value of the ICI shares, of 6.3 per cent per annum between 31 March 1982 and 30 December 1992, was 2.3 points lower than the *target growth*. In other words, the ICI share price, over this period, showed only a moderate real growth and did not match the All Share Index. If the shares had been purchased on 31 December 1986, however, they would have lost 5.6 per cent per annum in real value by 30 December 1992, whereas they would have grown in real value by

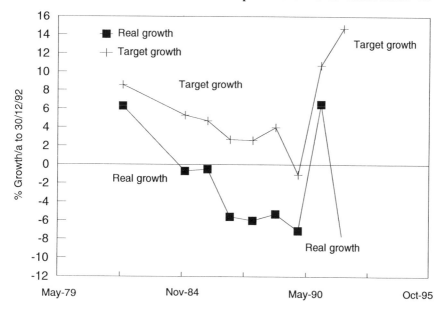

Figure 4.2   ICI shares: growth rates over periods to 30/12/92

2.7 per cent if they had tracked the All Share Index. On the other hand, purchase on 28 December 1990 would have resulted in a *real growth* of 25.6 per cent per annum by 3 April 1992, compared with a *target growth* of only 3.5 per cent per annum; a result of the Hanson initiative already mentioned. (Since then Hanson is reported to have sold his 20 million shares at £14 per share, having bought them at £11.94, possibly foreseeing the very slow recovery in the economy that has been experienced up to the time of writing). Since the earlier part of 1992, ICI shares have lost real value whilst the *target growth* has been excellent. The gross yield on 27 December 1991 was 6.5 per cent. The higher than target figure indicates that the possibility of a takeover bid had not fully overcome doubts about the future profitability of ICI. By 30 December 1992 the gross *yield* had increased to 6.9 per cent, more than 50 per cent higher than the *target yield*, as all hope of a takeover bid had disappeared.

The most concise assessment of the medium to long term performance of a share is achieved by measuring the real rate of return of the share. The return depends on both the growth in the share price and the dividends paid. The figures for ICI shares are shown in Table 4.1; the *real return* has seriously under-performed the *target return* over the review period, particularly over the last year, when the figures were −3 per cent per annum and 18 per cent per annum respectively.

In view of the conclusions drawn from the data in Table 4.1 and the fact that the gross yield has been in the 4 to 8 per cent range over the review period, compared with the *target yield* of 4 to 6 per cent, it can be concluded that ICI shares were a moderate investment if they were purchased in the early 1980s, or between late 1990 and early 1991. Purchase at other times would have resulted in a loss in value in real terms, although it must be said that for much of this period the average share also lost value. Only over the early years of the review period and around late 1990 has the *real return* to 30 December 1992 exceeded that achieved by the three-month inter-bank rate (see Table 13.1). The optimum performance would have been achieved if the shares had been sold in the mid-1980s and the proceeds invested in a fixed income security of some kind.

Readers are reminded that this chapter has been written to demonstrate the application of the System of share performance measurement to an individual, i.e. an ICI share. To make the example as meaningful as possible, and avoid unecessary complication, the review was terminated on 30 December 1992, before the demerger divided ICI into two companies, ICI and Zeneca. As already mentioned, the more recent figures can be found in Table 13.3 on the floppy disk.

PORTFOLIO PERFORMANCE

In the System proposed in this book, the performance of a portfolio of shares is assessed by measuring the same criteria as were used to assess the medium to long-term performance of individual shares, i.e. the *real growth*, yield and *real return*, and the corresponding targets.

A portfolio of 12 shares has been constructed to allow the System of portfolio performance measurement to be explained and demonstrated. A detailed description and performance assessment of this *selected portfolio* is given in Chapter 11 and Table 13.4; the figures are summarised in Table 11.13 and the graph in Figure 11.1. A brief mention of the key performance figures is included here to engage the reader's interest, the end date of the review period being 30 December 1992. The real value of the *selected portfolio* has grown at only 6.5 per cent per annum over the more than 10 years of the review period, compared with the *target* of 8.6 per cent per annum. Over shorter periods the growth has been even lower, and indeed has been negative over the three years since the year-end 1989. The yield has been equal to or slightly in excess of the *target yield* throughout the period. The *real return* was 8 per cent per annum over the last eight years, falling to 1 per cent per annum over the last three years and then rising to 23 per cent per annum over the last year. The corresponding *target returns* were 9, 3 and 18 per cent per annum respectively. Inspection of these figures leads to the conclusion that the overall performance of the *selected portfolio* can be classified as satisfactory.

5

HOW TO CALCULATE THE PERFORMANCE OF INDIVIDUAL SHARES

'A thing may look specious in theory, and yet be ruinous in practice; a thing may look evil in theory, and yet be in practice excellent.'
Edmund Burke, 1729 – 1797

GENERAL

Share price and yield

The ways in which the performance criteria are calculated for an individual share are described in this chapter. It has already been mentioned that two different groups of criteria of share price performance are used in the recommended System, one primarily for the short-term and the other for the longer-term. The short-term performance of individual shares is assessed by comparing the movement of the share price with the movement of the FT-A All Share Index (AlShI). Graphing the share price, Retail Price Index and All Share Index was shown, in Figure 4.1, to be an unsatisfactory method for assessing performance. A better method is to monitor the ratio of the share price to the All Share Index. Movements in this ratio, which, after rebasing to 1.0 is called the *P/A ratio*, are an important indication of whether the price of each share is performing better or worse than average. Two other criteria used to assess performance are the P/E ratio and the dividend yield, the standard of comparison for the latter being the yield of the All Share Index, i.e. the *target yield*. P/E ratios were not available for the companies included in the All Share Index as a whole until recently, so target P/E ratios have not been used as standards in the System. They could, however, be included in the future, especially in view of the attempt the accountancy profession is now making to ensure a standard approach by all companies to the calculation of earnings per share. Some investors might decide to record the P/E ratio of the companies in the 500-Share Index, and use it as a basis for comparison. The other information required when considering whether to sell a holding of shares is the potential liability to capital gains tax (CGT), and for this purpose the *real gain* is also monitored at frequent intervals. The longer-term performance of individual shares is assessed by measuring the *real growth*, and comparing this with the growth that would have been achieved if the share price had tracked the All Share Index, i.e with the *target growth*. The pattern of movement of the yield is also important and must be monitored. The *real return* is also measured; the method of calculation is described in the section in this chapter on the rate of return on an investment in a share

In general, the price of a share will move up or down in line with the All Share Index when there is no new information emerging concerning the particular share being studied or the sector within which it operates. Under these circumstances the movement of the share price will depend on the changing view of the economic, business and political prospects in the country. These same variables will also influence all the other shares, so that even though the price of a particular share might move up or down by a considerable amount, the *P/A ratio* will remain constant. A share having had a history of constant *P/A ratios* can be said to have experienced an average investment performance. It follows that when a significant movement takes place in the *P/A ratio*, it will usually have been caused by a change in the perception some investors have of the future prospects of the company. This can be a consequence of changes in the future prospects of either the sector, the company's competitors or the company itself as a result, for instance, of the publishing of an annual or half-yearly report. Inside information, available only to a limited number of investors, can also influence the share price and hence the *P/A ratio*. This is, of course, why the media publish information about the purchases and sales of a company's shares by directors of the company.

Investors with large portfolios of shares might choose to analyse their shares after dividing them into the *Financial Times* company classifications, i.e. capital goods, consumer group, etc. The appropriate index could then be used for each company classification, instead of the All Share Index. This approach will not be considered further, as the extra complication will not be worthwhile for the great majority of private investors, although they would be well advised to make themselves aware of the relative movements in the equity groups and sub-sections of the All Share Index.

It must also be pointed out that there are good arguments for using the All Share Index as the universal target, even for large portfolios. After all, if an investor invests in a sector which underperforms the All Share Index, it is right that the performance analysis should identify this underperformance, since the investor chose to invest in that sector, rather than a sector which might have performed better than the All Share Index. The adoption of the All Share Index as a universal standard, both for individual shares and for portfolios, has the advantage not only of avoiding complication, but also of ease of understanding and calculation.

It is worth pointing out here that there is not necessarily a direct correlation, over the short-term, between the price of a company's shares and its profitability. A company can, for instance, publish its latest results showing an increase in profits of, say, 30 per cent only to find that the price of its shares falls in the market. The explanation is generally that the market had anticipated an increase in company profits of, say, 50 per cent and been disappointed when the increase was only 30 per cent. In these circumstances the yield on the share would have been low relative to the *target yield*. The publication of the 30 per cent profit increase would have been expected to lead to an increse in the yield.

Effect of inflation

A more complete picture of the performance of a share is only revealed, however, by considering the relationship of the share price to the Retail Price Index as well as to the All Share Index. By buying at the bottom of a recession, for instance, although the *P/A ratio* might remain constant over future years, the real value of the share would be expected to increase (the All Share Index will be increasing fairly rapidly whereas the Retail Price Index will normally be increasing quite slowly after a recession, compared with previous years). On the other hand, if the shares had been purchased at the peak of the market, the value of the shares would be expected to fall in real terms, although the *P/A ratio* remained constant. The performance assessment therefore calculates the *real growth* in the share price on each of the dates in the review period (see the section in this chapter on the real growth of the share price).

A knowledge of how the All Share Index and the Retail Price Index have moved in the past can be important in deciding whether the time has come to change the balance in the investor's portfolio between the different categories of investment. A sustained fall in the All Share Index can occur simultaneously with an acceleration in the rate of increase in the cost of living (i.e. the Retail Price Index), a combination often associated with the onset of a recession. The prudent investor, who detects the early warning signs of a recession, might well then consider selling some shares, particularly those of companies normally badly hit by recessions, in order to invest in fixed interest securities.

Price/earnings ratio and cover

The figures for the price/earnings ratio are available from the newspapers and should also be reviewed, as they can assist in understanding past and future performance. The cover is not an independent variable, in that it can be expressed as a function of the yield and the P/E ratio; i.e.

$$\text{Cover} = 100 / (\text{P/E Ratio} \times \text{Net Yield})$$

In assessing the performance of a share, therefore, it is important to review the yield and the P/E ratio. Whether to include the cover in the data to be reviewed is a matter of personal choice by the investor.

The P/E ratio, and therefore the cover, do have the disadvantage that their calculation depends on the particular accountancy conventions adopted by the company, as do many of the figures that can be obtained from the company report to shareholders. The way in which exceptional and extraordinary items are dealt with, for instance, can have a major influence on the underlying meaning of the figure reported for earnings per share and consequently P/E ratio and cover, although action is now being taken by the accountancy profession to improve reporting by introducing some new standards.

The future

Finally, readers are reminded that a share's price is determined by investors' beliefs about the future performance of the company as well as their knowledge of its past performance. Unfortunately the only firm information many investors have is about past performance. The company's annual and mid-term reports are generally vague and non-specific in their forecasts of the future. However unsatisfactory it is, then, to use a knowledge of past performance to help predict the future, such information is generally used by investors to assist in their buying and selling decisions. It is essential, therefore, for the investor to understand properly the past performance of the shares and this is one of the objectives of the System outlined in this book.

To conclude, the decision to buy or sell can be assisted by monitoring the *P/A ratio* and *real gain* at frequent intervals. This method is recommended as part of the System for the short-term assessment of share performance. A better understanding of the performance of a particular share, over the medium and long-term, can only be obtained, however, by reviewing the relationship between the price of the share and both the All Share Index and the Retail Price Index, and expressing the results in easily understood terms. This is achieved by calculating the *real growth* of each share, comparing the figures with the *target growth* and using this data, together with the dividend yield and the P/E ratio, to assess the performance of the share. An alternative measure of long-term performance is the *real return*, the standard of comparison being the *target return*.

CORRECTED SHARE PRICES

It is important, when monitoring the way share prices have moved over a range of dates, that the prices are meaningful. For this to be the case a correction has to be applied to allow for the effect of scrip issues.

Shares in this context are taken to include Unit Trusts (UT) and Investment Trusts (InvTr) as well as ordinary shares. In order to allow a valid comparison to be made the share price must be corrected for the issue of any scrip, bonus or capitalisation shares. For instance, if the number of shares held is doubled, without the need for any payment by the owner, as a result of a scrip issue by the company, the market price of each share will fall to half the previous figure, thereby maintaining the value of the holding of shares in the company. In the application of the System, therefore, the published prices (Pr) of the shares have been adjusted for scrip issues to obtain the *corrected price* (Pr(c)) and this *corrected price* is the one that is compared with the Index.

Table 5.1 Corrected share price

Date	No. of shares	Price/share pence	Cor'd price/sh. pence
8/10/91	1000	100	50
10/10/91	2000	50	50

Definition:
Pr(c) [8/10/91] = Pr[8/10/91] × No.[8/10/91] / No.[10/10/91]

The company in the example shown in Table 5.1 has, on the 9 October 1991, made a one for one scrip issue, so that the number of shares held has increased from 1,000 to 2,000 without any payment being required, and the price has consequently fallen from 100p to 50p. It is seen that the *corrected price* Pr(c) is the same as the actual quoted price on the latest date for which the figures are shown, i.e. 10 October 1991 in the above example. The *corrected price* is also the same as it was two days before, on 8 October 1991, despite the scrip issue having taken place. This is fundamentally the same method as that used in the *Financial Times* publication *CGT Capital Gains Tax*, which was published to give the key figures needed to calculate this tax, taking into account the 1988 budget capital gains tax (CGT) proposals. The key figures referred to in that publication are the *corrected prices* of shares and unit trusts on 31 March 1982, and the Capital Gains Tax Indexation Allowance figures in that month and subsequently. Updated values of the Capital Gains Tax Indexation Allowances, which are a function of the Retail Price Index, are frequently published in the financial press.

The share price should also theoretically be adjusted to take account of rights issues when calculating the *corrected price*. Such adjustments are only necessary when the issue price is significantly different from the current market price and the number of shares to be issued is a high proportion of the number of existing shares. The appropriate calculation is shown in Appendix 5. When a rights issue has been taken up the number of shares received and the cost are recorded in the *Mspdata file* (see Chapter 9 and, for the *selected portfolio*, Table 13.2), the cost contributing to the investment total. When the rights have not been taken-up, any cash received by the share holder from the proceeds of the sale of the shares not taken-up is recorded as a negative investment in the *Mspdata file*.

THE P/A RATIO OF A SHARE

How to calculate the P/A ratio

Changes in the price of a share, relative to the All Share Index, can be monitored by calculating the *P/A ratio*. In the example in Table 5.2 the ratios 'Price(c)/AlShI' are calculated first; in order to calculate the *P/A ratios*, these figures are then rebased by dividing them all by the 1990 'Price(c)/AlShI' ratio of 0.77. This results in a *P/A ratio* of 1.0 at the end of 1990 for all the shares.

An example of how the *P/A ratio* can be used to analyse the performance of a share is shown in Table 5.2.

Table 5.2 Calculation of P/A ratio

	Year end		1991		
	1989	1990	22/11	29/11	6/12
Price(c)	750	800	900	850	800
AlShI	1205	1038	1183	1169	1149
RPI	119.1	130.1	135.9	136.0	136.1
Price(c)/AlShI	0.62	0.77	0.76	0.73	0.70
P/A ratio	**0.81**	**1.00**	**0.99**	**0.94**	**0.90**
% Yield	3.2	3.5	3.5	4.3	5.0
% Target yield	4.2	5.4	5.0	5.1	5.2

Definitions:
a) Price Ratio = Price(c)/AlShI / re-basing constant
b) Rebasing constant = Price(c) (end 1990) / AlShI (end 1990)

The meaning of changes in *P/A ratio*

The *P/A ratios* in the example in Table 5.2. show that the price of the share under review, having grown significantly between 1989 and 1990 relative to the All Share Index, has started to fall during the period November to December 1991. Over the full period of the review, however, the *P/A ratio* has increased from 0.81 to 0.9.

Between the end of 1990 and 22 November 1991 the price increased from 800 to 900 whilst the Retail Price Index increased from 130.1 to 135.9. A quick mental calculation indicates that there was a real increase in the value of the shares over this period. The share value fell in real terms, however, from 22 November 1991 to 6 December 1991. These figures, together with the fact that the *P/A ratio* also fell over this period, would obviously lead investors to look for the reason for the fall and to consider whether to continue to hold these shares. Another point to note is the increase in the yield that has taken place, indicating that investors believe that this is no longer a share with above average growth potential. This example demonstrates that an inspection of the price and Retail Price Index figures can give an approximate indication of whether a share is increasing or decreasing in real value over the short-term. Assessing the relationship of the price to the Retail Price Index by a process of mental arithmatic is not satisfactory, however, so that for a performance analysis over the medium and longer-term it is best to calculate the *real growth*.

Comparing the *P/A ratio* of different shares

The System outlined above allows the performance of individual shares to be monitored, over a period of time, against the All Share Index. It also allows the performance of the shares to be compared, one with another, providing it is borne in mind that the other data known about the shares and, in particular, the dividend yield, must be included in the comparison. An extreme example of this is the type of unit trust where the income from dividends, instead of being distributed or being used to buy extra units, is reinvested in the trust to increase the value of the existing units, i.e. accumulation units. The distributed dividend yield is then zero and the share price of such units should obviously grow faster than normal units. Since the net dividend yield is normally in the range 3 to 4 per cent, the value of the unit trust (acc) units should grow faster than normal unit trusts by the same percentage (assuming standard rate tax on dividends and no CGT). Some unit trusts are available as either income units or accumulation units, depending on whether the net income is distributed or reinvested. If the accumulation units are held, some investors might decide to keep the prices of both types of units in their records. The price of the income units could then be used to calculate the *P/A ratios*.

   An example of some of the data collected for the assessment of the short-term performance of the individual shares in a portfolio is shown in Table 5.3. The dates are the same as those shown in Table 5.2 and the ratios for share A are those determined by the calculations demonstrated in Table 5.2.

   The System can accommodate the purchase of shares part way through the review period; an example is share C which was purchased during 1990. In such cases the ratios are rebased to 1.00

Table 5.3 Performance assessment by *P/A ratio*

				P/A ratio			*Latest*
			Year end		*1991*		*% yield*
		1989	*1990*	22/11	29/11	6/12	
Ordinary	A	0.81	1.00	0.99	0.94	0.90	5.0
Ordinary	B	1.10	1.00	0.90	0.90	0.90	4.5
Ordinary	C	1.10p	1.00	1.05	1.00	1.00	4.4
Unit Trust	D	0.75	1.00	1.00	0.98	1.00	3.5
Unit Tr(Acc)	E	0.92	1.00	1.07	1.07	1.10	0.0
							(4.0)
AlShI		1205	1038	1183	1169	1149	
RPI		119.1	130.1	135.9	136.0	136.1	

Definitions:

a) The use of the currency format (example 1.10p. for share C in Table 5.3) indicates that the figure is calculated from the purchase or selling price and is not the figure on the date shown at the top of the column.

b) The yield for share E must be taken as zero (see explanation above), for the purposes of this assessment, but the dividend, which has been reinvested after deduction of tax, is shown in brackets.

on the first record entry date after purchase or on the same date as that on which the other ratios are rebased, whichever is the later. In this case it is the end of 1990. The performance of share C can now be assessed over the period since purchase and compared with the performance of the other holdings over the same period. The *P/A ratio* in the 1989 column for share C is seen to be 1.10p. It is derived from the purchase price of the holding of 'C' shares, and uses the index on the date of purchase, rather than on the date at the top of the column, for the calculation of the *P/A ratio*. The currency format is also used when recording the corrected purchase price. These figures are inserted in the appropriate table, in the column for the period before the purchase took place and the 'p' is affixed to distinguish them from the other period-end figures. The entry in the Table for the *P/A ratio* for the newly purchased share is calculated as follows:

$$P/A \text{ ratio} = \frac{\text{Purchase price (c)}}{\text{AlShI (at purchase)}} \times \text{Rebasing constant}$$

This procedure allows the change that has taken place in the price of the shares between purchase and the first period-end entry to be evaluated. In the example in Table 5.3, this amounts to a loss of approximately 9 per cent for share C between the date of purchase and the end of 1990, some of the loss being accounted for by the costs involved in purchasing the shares.

Looking at Table 5.3 for shares where the *P/A ratio* has increased over the review period (end 1989 to 6 December 1991), it is seen that shares A, D and E have outperformed the All Share Index over the full period of the review, although this is an unfair comparison in the case of Share E, since the dividends of this share are reinvested. Only part of the increase in the *P/A ratio* of share E can be explained by the reinvestment, however. (The investor's taxation situation can often be the factor which would determine which share is the best, but this is unlikely in this case since the reinvested dividends (share E) are subject to the same taxation as the dividends of the other shares). Share B has underperformed the All Share Index by almost 20 per cent over the two years. The shares which have not performed well in terms of capital growth have the highest yields, as would be expected. In conclusion, the performance of each of the shares should be reviewed in the light of other information about the company (e.g. profitability or return on capital), to determine whether the price fully reflects the potential for growth of the company.

The decision as to whether to sell or buy would be assisted by knowing how the share prices were moving after taking inflation into account, and it is for this purpose that the Retail Price Index is recorded in Table 5.3. A mental calculation is needed to show that, between the end of 1990 and 6 December 1991, shares C, D and E all increased in real value. It would be possible to quantify the importance of the effect of inflation by calculating the ratio of the price to the Retail Price Index , but for the reasons outlined in Appendix 5 the development of the *real growth* method of assessment was the preferred option (see the section in this chapter on the real growth rate of the share price).

The use of the *P/A ratio* to monitor the performance of individual shares has been explained in this chapter. The reader is reminded, however, that the use of the *P/A ratios* is recommended primarily for monitoring short-term performance, although the principles apply equally to both the short and long-term. The longer-term perform-ance is best assessed by monitoring the *real growth*.

The frequency with which share prices are recorded is discussed in Chapter 9, but in the last resort it is a matter for individual judge-ment. *P/A ratios* are needed frequently for the recent past. *Real growth* and *target growth* figures are useful to have at, say, quarterly intervals over the most recent two years at least, and perhaps less frequently over the longer-term.

The file used to record the data and carry out the calculations described above for the individual shares is named 'Measuring Share Performance – Prices' (*MspPri*). Details of the file contents are given in Chapter 9, as are the details of the file carrying the basic informa-tion about the equity shares, 'Measuring Share Performance – Data' (*MspData*). *P/A ratios* for the shares in the *selected portfolio* are to be found in Table 13.3.

CAPITAL GAINS TAX

The way in which the *P/A ratio* can be used to assist in reaching decisions on buying or selling shares has been outlined above. Another factor of importance in such decision making is the potential liability to CGT. The System, therefore, incorporates the regular production of the data necessary to estimate any liability to CGT on the sale of a share holding, i.e. the *real gain*, which is the gain in the share price after taking inflation into account. The principles on which the data are based are now discussed, followed by the example in Table 5.4.

The *real gain* provides information on the composition of the market price (normally just called the price) of the share on any selected date. The *inflated price* is the start price increased in line with inflation. The *real gain* is the difference between the price and the *inflated price*. The diagram that follows and Figure 5.1 can help in understanding this concept.

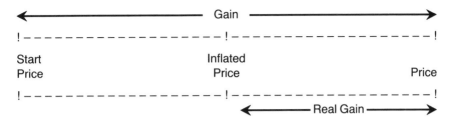

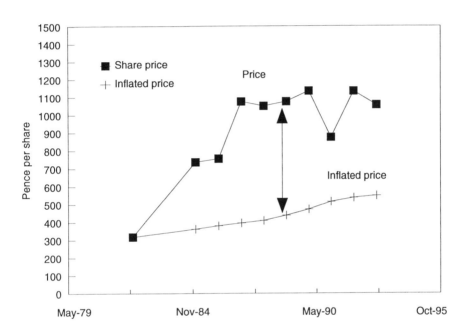

Figure 5.1   ICI shares: real gain in share price from 31/3/82

Figure 5.1 shows graphically the *real gain* of the ICI shares, the figures being extracted from the data in Table 4.1. (The graph does not represent the data in the example in Table 5.4).

The share price at purchase is called the start price, unless the shares were purchased before 31 March 1982, in which case the start price is the *corrected price* on that day, in accordance with the CGT regulations. In the example in Table 5.4, the shares were assumed to have been purchased at the end of 1986.

Table 5.4 Individual shares: real gain and CGT

Year end	1986	1987	1988	1989
Price(c),p./share	500	550	600	775
AlShI	833	891	926	1205
P/A ratio	0.93	0.96	1.01	1.00
RPI	100	103.3	110.6	119.1
Infl price,p./share	500	517	553	596
Real gain,p./share		34	47	180
Real gain,£		1675	2350	8975

Definitions:

a) The start date is the date of purchase and is end-1986.

b) In the equations below, 'y' indicates the date at the top of the column.

c) Infl(ated) Price (y) = Price (start) × RPI (y) / RPI (start).

d) Real gain, p/share = Price − Infl price.

e) Real gain, £ = Real gain, p./share × Number of shares / 100.

f) Number of shares assumed is 5,000.

The gain between 1986 and 1989 = (775 − 500) = 275 pence/share. This figure can be deceptive, however, unless the extent to which the price has increased in value due to inflation is known. The recommended System therefore uses the criterion *real gain*, which is the gain in the share price after taking inflation into account. The *inflated price* is defined as the start price corrected to show its equivalent purchasing power at a later date. Examples of some of the calculations used to construct Table 5.4 are shown below:

$$\text{Infl price}(1989) = \text{Price(start)} \times \text{RPI}(1989) / \text{RPI(start)}$$
$$= 500 \times 119.1 / 100 = 596\text{p}.$$

The *real gain* on a particular date is defined as the difference between the price on that date and the *inflated price* on the same date. The figures for the end of 1989 are:

$$\text{Real gain} = \text{Price} - \text{Infl price} = 775 - 596 = 180\text{p}.$$

The figures in the example in Table 5.4 show a progressive increase in the *real gain* of the shares, at the end of each of the years 1987 to 1989, of 34p, 47p and 180p respectively.

The *real gain,£* of the share holding is calculated from the *real gain,p* of the individual share as follows:

Real gain,£ = Real gain (pence/share) × No. of shares / 100

The *real gain* at the end of 1989 is therefore:

$$180 \times 5,000 / 100 = £8,975$$

Regular monitoring of the *real gain,£* is important, in that it is an approximation of the figure on which CGT will be paid if the shares are sold (after deducting the exemption limit of £5,000 in 1989/90, of course). The accurate figure for CGT liability is calculated from ratios published by the Government, which are a function of the Retail Price Index for the month of purchase and the month of sale; transaction costs are allowed. The figure calculated by the System is accurate enough, however, to give a warning of when a sale might incur CGT. It has been shown from the figures in Table 5.4 that the sale of the holding (assumed to comprise 5,000 shares) in 1989 would have incurred a *real gain* of £8,975, and therefore tax would have been payable on approximately (£8,975 − £5,000) = £3,975.

The calculations outlined above are based on the number of shares in the initial holding on the first purchase date, or on 31 March 1982, whichever is the later. Subsequent purchases of shares could also incur CGT if they were sold; the System does not produce early warning of this liability, so the investor must always keep this eventuality in mind.

THE REAL GROWTH RATE OF THE SHARE PRICE

The use of the *P/A ratio* to analyse performance must be regarded as an empirical device which allows an easy and quick assessment to be made of share performance. It is not a fundamental piece of information about a share, as is the real rate of growth, for instance. The use the *real growth*, and comparison with the *target growth*, are therefore recommended as part of the System for the measurement of the performance of both individual shares and portfolios, over the medium and longer-term. The yield must also be taken into account, of course, and also for comparison the *target yield*. An overall assessment of performance can then be achieved by calculating the *real return* and, for comparison, the *target return*.

Calculation of the real growth rate

The first task in the measurement of the *real growth* of a share is to calculate the rate of growth of the share price and the Retail Price Index (i.e. the rate of inflation). The rate of growth over a period greater than one year is the compound rate, which is calculated very easily using the Lotus spreadsheet @RATE Function or compound interest tables. The *real growth* is determined by calculation from the price growth rate and rate of inflation. The method of calculation is shown for an individual share in the example in Table 5.5 below, using the same share prices and dates as in Table 5.4. A summary of the main definitions follows the Table. Further details of the definitions and proofs are to be found in Appendix 2.

Table 5.5   Individual shares: real growth rates

Year end	1986	1987	1988	1989
Price(c),p/share	500	550	600	775
RPI	100	103.3	110.6	119.1
Annual rate to end 1989				
% Inflation	6.0	7.4	7.7	
% Price growth	15.7	18.7	29.2	
% Real growth	**9.2**	**10.6**	**19.9**	
% Divi yield		3.0	3.2	3.2

Definitions:
a) 'x' and 'y' are dates at the tops of columns.
b) The definition of % growth/a, when the period over which the growth is being measured is more than one year, is the compound growth rate. Using the Lotus spreadsheet function:

% Price growth p.a. = @Rate(Price(y),Price(x),No.of years)

The % Inflation p.a. (Infl) can be calculated in the same way:
Infl = @Rate(RPI(y),RPI(x),No. of years).

c) %Real growth = $100 \times (\%\text{Price growth} - \text{Infl})/(100 + \text{Infl})$

Examples follow of the calculations of the figures in Table 5.5, for the period from the end of 1986 to the end of 1989:

$$\% \text{ Inflation} = @\text{Rate}(119.1, 100.0, 3) = 6.0\,\%$$

$$\% \text{ Price growth} = @\text{Rate}(775, 500, 3) = 15.7\,\%$$

$$\% \text{ Real growth} = 100 \times (15.7 - 6.0)/(100 + 6.0) = 9.2\,\%$$

Calculation of the target growth rate

Table 5.6 shows the same figures as those in Table 5.5, plus the figures needed to calculate the target growth rate, which is, of course, the *real growth* that would have been achieved if the share price had tracked the All Share Index. The *target growth*, on any particular date, is independent of the price of the share, being derived from the All Share Index growth rate and the rate of inflation. It is a function only of the Retail Price Index and the All Share Index, and is therefore the same for all shares, varying only with the first and last dates of the period over which the growth rate is being measured. The dividend yield can be compared with the *target yield*, which is the yield of the shares in the All Share Index and is therefore the yield the share would have had if it had tracked the All Share Index.

Table 5.6 Individual shares: real and target growths

Year end	1986	1987	1988	1989
Price(c),p.	500	550	600	775
Index(RPI)	100	103.3	110.6	119.1
Index(AlShI)	833	891	926	1205
Annual rate to end 1989				
% Inflation	6.0	7.4	7.7	
% AlShI growth	13.1	16.3	30.1	
% Price growth	15.7	18.7	29.2	
% Real growth	**9.2**	**10.6**	**19.9**	
% Targ growth	**6.7**	**8.3**	**20.8**	
% Divi yield (net)		3.0	3.2	3.2
% Targ yield (net)		3.1	3.5	3.2

Definitions:
a) % AlShI growth/a = @Rate(AlShI(y), AlShI(x), No. of years)
b) % Targ growth/a = 100 × (% AlShI growth/a − Infl)/(100+Infl)

Examples follow of the calculations of the figures in Table 5.6, for the period from the end of 1986 to the end of 1989:

$$\% \text{ AlShI growth} = @\text{Rate}(1205,833,3) = 13.1\,\%$$

$$\% \text{ Targ growth} = 100 \times (13.1 - 6.0) / (100 + 6.0) = 6.7\,\%$$

Interpretation of the real and target growth rates

In the example in Table 5.6 the *real growth/a* over the three years was 9.2 per cent whilst the *target growth/a*, over the same three years, was 6.7 per cent, indicating that the increase in the share price was significantly better than if the price had tracked the All Share Index. In other words, if the share price had tracked the All Share Index the real value of the shares would have risen by 6.7 per cent per annum, whereas in fact the share price grew in real terms by 9.2 per cent per annum.

The figures in Table 5.6 show a progressive improvement in the *real growth/a* from 9.2 per cent over three years to 10.6 per cent over two years and 19.9 per cent over the last year. Comparison of the *target growth* and *real growth* figures shows that the share performed better than the All Share Index over the full period of the review (three years), and over two years, but that the position was reversed over the last year.

The yield was only marginally lower than target in each of the three years of the review. The overall conclusion is that the share has performed better than the average share. This relationship is quantified by calculating the *real return*, as described in the next section of this chapter (the rate of return on investment in a share).

Comparing the growth rates of different shares

For shares purchased on a date within the review period, *real growth* should be calculated over the period from the date of purchase to the end of the review period, as well as over the selected periods for which share prices are recorded. An example of this method can be seen in Table 5.7 where the performance of a number of shares is analysed.

Table 5.7 Performance of shares and portfolios

	% Real growth/a over years to end 1991			% yield (gross) at year end		
	7	*4*	*1*	*1985*	*1988*	*1991*
Ordinary						
Share A	3.0	−4.0	9.0	6.0	6.0	6.9
Share B	12.1	2.4	15.5	3.2	3.1	4.0
Avg.(Ord)	7.6	−0.8	12.3	4.6	4.6	5.5
Unit trusts						
UT C	6.5	−0.5	12.0	4.4	4.5	5.3
UT (Acc)D	8.0	1.5	15.1	(3.1)	(3.2)	(3.50)
UT E		1.3	14.5		3.8	5.0
Avg.(UTs)	7.3	0.8	13.9	2.2	2.8	3.4
Avg(All)	7.4	0.1	13.2	3.4	3.5	4.2
Target	7.2	−0.8	12.8	4.4	4.2	5.4

The growth figures are analysed over the last seven, four and one year(s) in Table 5.7. These intervals are a matter of personal choice and could, for instance, have been at regular one yearly intervals. The unit trust E was purchased after the start of the review period. It is useful to know the *real growth* since the date of purchase as well as on the chosen dates for data entry, and the calculation of these figures is included in the System. Because the date of purchase was different to the chosen dates, the *target growth* must be calculated for this specific purchase date, to establish a valid standard of comparison for the *real growth* since purchase. The starting data in the equations comprises the price, RPI and AlShI on the date of purchase. The *real growth* of share E since purchase was 5.0 per cent per annum, whilst the target was 3.6 per cent per annum. When comparing the perform-ance of the shares, differences in the *yield* must, of course, be taken into account, as well as the growth in the share price.

Share D is an unit trust(acc.) in which the net dividends are automatically reinvested, thereby causing the value of the units to increase. An assessment of its performance must take note of the fact that the growth in the value of the units will be expected to be higher than for normal unit trusts, to compensate for the fact that the dividend distributed is zero. Putting brackets around the yields indi-cates that no dividends were distributed to shareholders.

Over seven years ordinary share B performed best, whilst A was the poorest, the three unit trusts occupying the middle position (taking account of the zero yield for UT D). The same ranking applies over four years and one year. The only share to significantly beat the All Share Index over the full seven years was B, although the fact that the yield was lower than target reduces some of the benefit. Two shares, share A and share D, significantly underperformed the All Share Index.

THE RATE OF RETURN ON AN INVESTMENT IN A SHARE

Assessing the performance of shares in terms of the real growth rate of the share price and the yield has been chosen for inclusion in the System. This method is at its weakest, however, when it is used to compare the performance of investments with widely different yields, or when comparing normal unit trusts with those of the accumulative type. The comparison is assisted in cases such as these by the use of the real return on investment. The total real return on investment takes into account both the real increase in the capital invested (i.e. the share price), and the net dividends. The use of the prefix 'real', as elsewhere in the book, indicates that the return is calculated after taking inflation into account. The System defines the *real return* of an individual share, over a particular period, as the addition of the *real growth* and the yield (net), (see Appendix 2). The yield (net) is calculated as the average of the net yields over the chosen period. This is a simplification of the true relationship between these variables, but is sufficiently accurate for our purposes, as demonstrated in Appendix 4. In recognition of the lack of exactness in the calculation, *real returns* will only be reported in round numbers.

The general equation, as just defined, is:

$$\% \text{ Real return/a} = \% \text{ Real growth/a} + \% \text{ Yield(net)}$$

Accumulation unit trusts are a special case because the net dividends are reinvested to increase the price of the units, rather than to buy further units. Because no dividend is received from an Unit Trust (Acc), the yield is zero and therefore the *real growth* is equal to the *real return*. The standard of comparison for the *real growth* of Unit Trust (Acc) shares is therefore the *target return*.

An example of the use of the *real return* is shown in Table 5.8. The figures are abstracted from those in Table 5.7, and consider only the results over the period end 1984 to end 1991. Share E was not included because it was purchased less than seven years ago. The use of the *real return* makes it easier to rank the performances of the different shares.

The *target return* is defined as the addition of the *target growth* and the average *target yield* (net). It provides a standard of comparison for the *real return*, based on the All Share Index (price index and yield). The accuracy would have been improved if more yields had been included in the average.

Table 5.8 The *real return* on investment over a period of seven years to the end of 1991

	%Real growth p.a.	Avg.% net Yield	%Real return p.a.
Ordinary			
A	3.0	4.7	8
B	12.1	2.6	15
Avg.(Ord)	7.6	3.7	11
Unit Trusts			
C	6.5	3.6	10
D	8.0	0.0	8
Avg.(UT)	7.3	1.8	9
Avg.(All)	7.4	2.7	10
Target	7.2	3.5	11

The conclusions reached from an inspection of the *real growths* and the yields in Table 5.7 are confirmed by the *real return* figures shown above in Table 5.8, but the use of the *real return* makes it easier to arrive at this assessment. Both methods of assessment of share performance are included in the System. The record, over a period of time, of the *real growth* of the share price and the yield gives a detailed picture of performance, whilst the *real return* is used where simplicity is an advantage or where investments with appreciably different yields are being compared. The *real return* is particularly useful for comparing different types of investment, e.g. shares with fixed interest.

It might seem that the *real return* would be the only criterion needed for monitoring the medium to long-term share performance. The System, however, also recommends the use of the *real growth* and the yield to assess the performance of individual ordinary shares, as well as the *real return*. The reasons for this are:

a)   The way in which the yield changes over a period of time, in comparison with the *target yield*, can give additional information about the performance of the share that is not obvious from an inspection of the *real return* alone. For instance, the *real return* of a share might be constant over a period, although the yield has been increasing relative to the *target yield*. This piece of information would ring a warning bell in an investor's mind and cause him to look at the company's share and financial performance in more detail than would otherwise have been the case.

b)   For taxation reasons some investors will favour capital growth rather than income, whilst others will take the opposite point of view. Monitoring the *real growth* and the yield, rather than the *real return*, gives more information to investors who have a range of taxation objectives.

c)   The System produces accurate figures for the *real growth* and the *yield* of a share, but the *real return* is only an approximation.

To conclude, the calculation and recording of the *real growth*, yield and *real return*, are included in the recommended System for monitoring the performance of individual shares, over the medium to long-term.

6

HOW TO CALCULATE THE PERFORMANCE OF PORTFOLIOS

'Money is like muck, not good unless it be spread.'
Francis Bacon, 1561–1626

There are only three criteria used by the System for monitoring the performance of a portfolio, in contrast to the six used for individual shares. They are:

Yield
Real growth
Real return

The target growth and *target return* are calculated to establish standards for the principal criteria, *real growth* and *real return*. These can each be calculated in three different ways. These are:

Real growth
Average of *real growths* of individual shares.
Direct calculation of *real growth* by trial and error (T&E) method.
Calculation of *real growth* from *real return* and yield by internal rate of return (IRR) method.

Real return
Average of *real returns* of individual shares.
Direct calculation of *real return* by IRR method.
Calculation of *real return* from *real growth* and yield (T&E method).

The averaging method is not valid, for reasons explained later, but can provide information that is useful in explaining why a portfolio has performed in a certain way. The third of the methods listed above for calculating each of the principal criteria, *real growth* and *real return*, is simpler than the direct methods, but is not as accurate. It depends on the following approximate equation:

$$\% \ real \ return = \% \ real \ growth + \text{yield (net)}$$

Nevertheless, this method of calculation could be quite accurate enough for many investors. If this alternative is chosen, then it would only be necessary to calculate one of the two principal criteria by the direct method; the other principal criterion could be calculated using the above equation. This alternative is attractive because the calculations of both the principal criteria, and particularly the *real growth* by the T&E method, are more time-consuming than any others used by the System. The relative merits of the alternatives are discussed in the section on choice of methods, later in this chapter.

The ways in which the two principal criteria are calculated, by the direct methods, are described in the sections on the % growth of a portfolio and the % real return of a portfolio, the first of these dealing with the calculation of the *real growth*. The mathematics involved are very simple but somewhat laborious; to put this in perspective, the calculation could take a few minutes, and is only laborious when compared with, say, the calculation of the growth of a share, which is achieved by using the RATE function in seconds rather than minutes. It is recommended that the next section is read carefully, even though the reader might have no intention of using the direct method (T&E) for calculating the *real growth*. The reason for this recommendation is that it will lead to a much better understanding of the principles of portfolio performance measurement. The section on the real return of a portfolio describes the way the *real return* is calculated by the direct method (the IRR method).

DEFINITION OF A PORTFOLIO

A portfolio is simply a holding of shares in more than one company. Just as investors will want to measure the performance of each of their shares, so they will want to measure the performance of the whole portfolio as a single entity. Those portfolios that contain the shares of only a handful of 'companies' can be analysed as a single portfolio. Investors will probably prefer to divide larger portfolios into categories according to the type of investment, e.g. ordinary shares, unit trusts, unit trusts (accumulation units), investment trusts, Peps and fixed interest stocks. The performance of each category portfolio can then be analysed as well as the whole portfolio.

Ordinary and investment trust shares, and unit trust and unit trust (acc) units are all included in the category of shares in this book. The shares together with the Peps comprises the equity category and this together with the fixed interest stock comprises the investment category. For the purpose of simplicity, any investment that pays a fixed rate of interest is termed a stock and is put into the fixed interest category (despite the fact that preference shares are more correctly termed equity). There are a small number of unit trusts dealing in fixed interest securities only; these should be included in the fixed interest category and not the unit trust category.

Table 6.1 Categories of investment

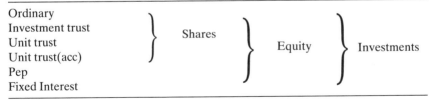

| Ordinary |
| Investment trust |
| Unit trust |
| Unit trust(acc) |
| Pep |
| Fixed Interest |

AVERAGE OF THE REAL GROWTH OF SHARES IN A PORTFOLIO

An estimation of the *real growth* of a portfolio can be obtained by averaging the *real growths* of the individual shares. In the same way the *real return* of the portfolio can be calculated by averaging the *real returns* of the individual shares. An example of how the performance of different shares can be compared was discussed in Chapter 5 and shown in Tables 5.7 and 5.8, using the calculations demonstrated in Tables 5.5 and 5.6. Also shown in Table 5.7 is the method for assessing the performance of category portfolios and the whole portfolio, by calculating the average of the *real growths* of each share. The following conclusions can be drawn from a review of the figures in the example in Table 5.7. The ordinary shares had a higher yield than the unit trusts, but the *real growths* were similar, slightly favouring the ordinary shares over the longer term and the unit trusts over the shorter term.

It is apparent that the overall performance of the ordinary shares was indistinguishable from that of the unit trusts. The average *real growth/a* for the whole portfolio over the seven years was 0.2 per cent higher than the target, but the average dividend yield was 2.5 per cent compared with the target of 3.8 per cent. It can be concluded, therefore, that the performance of the whole portfolio was worse than the target.

A simpler alternative to the one just described is to measure the average of the *real return* for each category of shares. This was done in Table 5.8. A comparison of the relative performance of each category can then be accomplished.

These two methods of assessing the performance of a portfolio, or comparing the performances of different categories of share within the portfolio, is seen to be staightforward and useful in checking on the investor's choice of shares. It has, however, the following important disadvantages.

a) It gives the same weighting to each share. An extreme example will demonstrate the importance of this weakness. Suppose a portfolio consists of two shares, A and B, the *real return* of A being 2 per cent per annum and that of B, 20 per cent per annum. If the value of the two share holdings is roughly equal, as is assumed by the average method, then the average of 11 per cent per annum would correctly represent the *real return* of the portfolio. On the other hand, if the A shares were worth 100 times the B shares, the *real return* of the portfolio would be only a fraction over 2 per cent per annum, compared with the average of 11 per cent per annum.

b) The average method cannot satisfactorily accommodate the purchase or sale of shares part-way through the period of the review. This is primarily because no account can be taken of any change that might take place in the share price between the date of purchase or sale and the next routine entry date.

c) It takes no account of the costs of buying or selling.

To conclude, monitoring the average of the *real growths* or *real returns* of the individual shares in a portfolio can give a misleading impression of the performance of the portfolio as a whole, mainly due to the fact that the average gives equal weight to each holding in the portfolio. In practice each holding will be of different value and a valid assessment of performance requires more importance or weight to be put on the larger holdings. The size of the holdings also changes with time, as shares are bought and sold. It is obvious that a better method is needed to assess the performance of a portfolio of shares than the use of the average. The method chosen for the System, which is not invalidated by the weaknesses just outlined, calculates the rate of real growth or real return of the portfolio as a whole and compares it with the rate of real growth/return that would have been obtained if the shares had grown in line with the All Share Index; i.e. the target growth or target return.

Despite its weaknesses, the average method is useful for helping in the interpretation of the portfolio performance figures, and has therefore been included in the System.

The data and calculations leading to the average *real return* figures for the *selected portfolio* are contained in the file 'Measuring Share Performance – Price', (*MspPri*), and in Table 13.3

THE GROWTH OF A PORTFOLIO

In the same way as the performance of a share can be measured in terms of the rate of growth of the price of the share and the yield, so the performance of a portfolio can be measured in terms of the rate of growth of the value of the portfolio and the yield. Although the principles behind the methods adopted for measuring the growth rates of individual shares and portfolios are the same, the detailed method of analysis outlined in Chapter 5, for measuring the rates of growth of individual shares, is not valid for portfolios because money is being moved into and out of the portfolio at intervals as a result of share purchases and sales. It is not possible, therefore, to calculate the % growth per annum of a portfolio from its starting value, end value and the years between the start and end of the review period, as was the case for an individual share. This section describes the direct method of calculating the rate of growth of a portfolio. The next section describes how the real growth rate of the portfolio is calculated, from a knowledge of its growth rate and the rate of inflation. The next section also describes the calculation of the target growth rate. A more detailed explanation and proofs of these equations are given in Appendix 3.

Growth rate over part year

The growth rate of a portfolio, when there is no investment between the start date (x) and the end date (x+1), is as follows, 'Port' representing the value of the portfolio:

$$\% \text{ Port growth/a} = 100 \times (\text{Port}(x+1) - \text{Port}(x)) / \text{Port}(x)$$

This is essentially the same equation as was used to calculate the growth rate of the price of a share, but it requires modification if an investment has taken place, i.e. if shares have either been purchased or sold within the review period. The date on which the investment (Inv) takes place also affects the calculation of the growth rate. To give an example, the growth rate of £100 invested on 31 December 1990, and growing to £120 by 31 December 1991, would be 20 per cent per annum. If the investment had taken place at the beginning of 1990, however, instead of at the end, the growth rate would only have been 10 per cent per annum. The method of calculation of the portfolio growth rate must therefore take into account the actual date of any investment, rather than just the year in which it took place. This is achieved, whilst keeping the calculations simple, by the use of a variable called the *investment fraction*.

   When an investment (Inv) takes place D days before the end of the year, the investment, by definition, grows at the same rate (Gr) as the original portfolio, but only for a fraction D/365 of the year. The term *invested fraction* (InvFrac) is defined as:

$$InvFrac = Inv \times D / 365$$

The equation used to calculate the portfolio growth rate (*%Port growth/a*) is modified in the following way to take account of the investment in the portfolio (see Appendix 3):

%Port growth/a $= 100 \times (Port(x+1) - Port(x) - Inv) / (Port(x) + InvFrac)$

In the example in Table 6.2, which demonstrates the calculation of the growth rate over the past year and uses the above equation, the investment was assumed to be made 250 days from the end of the year (i.e. D = 250).

Table 6.2 Portfolios – % growth over past year.

Year end	1987	1988	1989	1990
Investment,£			300	
Inv Frac			205	
Port value,£	1000	1100	1700	1500
Past Year, %Port growth/a.		10.0	23.0	−11.8

Definitions:

a) x represents the date at the top of the columns. The date (x+1) represents the date one year later than x.

b) Inv Frac = Inv × D / 365 = 300 × 250/365 = 205

c) %Port growth/a = 100 × (Port(x+1)−Port(x)−Inv) / (Port(x)+Inv frac)

The growth rate for the year 1989 is calculated as follows:

$$Port\ growth/a = 100 \times (1700 - 1100 - 300) / (1100 + 205)$$
$$= 23.0\ \%$$

The advantage of the *invested fraction* method for calculating the growth rate of a portfolio is that the *invested fractions* of each share in each year can be added together, and the total used in the calculation of the portfolio growth rate.

Growth rate to end of review period

A full picture of the performance of the portfolio needs not only a knowledge of the growth rate over the past year, but also a knowledge of the growth rate from a range of dates up to the end of the review period. This in fact gives a better picture of the performance of the portfolio than the growth over the past year, which tends to vary widely from one year to the next. The equation required to calculate the growth rate (Gr) over the period from the date at the top of the column to the end of the period is derived in Appendix 3 and is:

$$Port(x+1) = Port(x) + Inv + Gr/100 \times (Port(x) + InvFract)$$

The growth rate is determined by the trial and error method, (referred to in future as the T&E method), as demonstrated in the calculations in Table 6.3.

Table 6.3 Portfolios – % growth to end of review period

%Growth/a		Year end	1987	1988	1989	1990
	Investment,£				300	
	Inv Frac				205	
	Port value,£		1000	1100	1700	1500
	Trial value,£					
5.4	Over 3 years		1000	1054	1422	1499
3.6	Over 2 years			1100	1447	1499
−11.8	Over 1 year				1700	1499

Definitions:

a) $Port(x+1) = Port(x) + Inv + Gr/100 \times (Port(x) + Inv\ Frac)$

Procedure

1) Calculate growth rate over three years, to the end of 1990:
   Make start trial value (1987) = Port value
   $$= £1,000$$
   Enter trial %Growth/a (in cell containing 5.4)
   Use above equation (definition a) to calculate trial values in 1988, then 1989 and finally 1990.
   Enter different trial growth rates until a figure of 5.4% results in

the trial value at end 1990 equalling the port value, (£1,500).

2) Calculate growth rate over two years, to the end of 1990:
Make start trial value (1988) = Port value
$$= £1,100$$
Enter trial %Growth/a (in cell containing 3.6)
Use above equation (definition a) to calculate trial values in 1989, then 1990.
Enter different trial growth rates until a figure of 3.6 per cent results in the trial value at end 1990 equalling Port value, (£1,500)

3) Calculate growth rate over one year, to the end of 1990:
Make start trial value (1989) = Port value
$$= £1,700$$
Enter trial %Growth/a (in cell containing −11.8)
Use above equation (definition a) to calculate trial value in 1990.
Enter different trial growth rates until a figure of −11.8 per cent results in the trial value at end 1990 equalling Port value, (£1,500).

In following the reasoning of the above calculations, the reader will find it of assistance to inspect the equations in Table 13.4(g) on the floppy disk. In the example in Table 6.3 a trial row in the spreadsheet is used for each starting year of the review period. In practice, all the calculations leading to the port growth rates can be accomplished by allocating two rows to the trial value figures. This is particularly valuable when the review period covers a large number of years. The first row, as is the case in Table 6.3, records the figures derived by applying the formulae already outlined to the calculation of the annual growth rate of the portfolio over the full review period. The figures in this row only change when a different trial % growth is inserted in the cell allocated for this purpose (the cell in the first column in Table 6.3, containing the number 5.4). The figures for the first of the trial and error calculations are reproduced in the first trial row in Table 6.3, showing that when a trial growth rate of 5.4 is entered, the 1990 trial value of £1,499 is equal (within £1) to the portfolio value of £1,500. The second trial row is copied from the first, thereby retaining in the first row the equations relating the trial value in any one year to that in the preceeding year; (the word 'copied' is used in the computer programming sense). This second row is used to calculate all the intermediate growth rates. For instance, the portfolio growth rate over the last two years, i.e. between 1988 and 1990, is calculated by entering the actual value of the portfolio at the end of 1988, £1,100, in the second trial row. Different growth rates are then entered in the cell reserved for this purpose in the first column until the figure of 3.6 is found to result in the 1990 trial value being equal to the portfolio value in the same year. The next step is to calculate the growth rate over one, i.e. the last, year, using the same procedure, i.e. the trial value at the end of 1989 is made equal to the portfolio value of £1,700 by entering this figure in the 1989 column in the second trial row. Application of the trial and error method then leads to a growth rate over one year of – 11.8 per cent. The effect of calculating the intermediate growth rates is to destroy some or all of the equations linking the trial values in the second trial row, but they are retained in the first trial row and can be recovered at any time by copying from the first row to the second. It is for this reason that two rows, rather than one, are used.

The use of two rows for the trial figures is shown in Table 6.4. Two cells contain the letters 'Gr'; the topmost of these is reserved for the entry of trial growth rates to allow the calculation of the growth rate over the full review period. The lower cell is for the entry of trial growth rates in the calculations of the intermediate growth rates.

THE REAL GROWTH OF A PORTFOLIO

The rate of growth in the value of an investment is one of the conventional performance criteria. A standard could be established in terms of the growth rate of the All Share Index, and termed the target. Some investors will choose not to take the next step, which is to correct the growth rate for the effects of inflation, but instead to use the conventional criteria to measure performance. It is a matter of personal choice, but, for the reasons already outlined, performance criteria expressed in terms of real growth or real return are recommended and included in the System. Those investors who intend to use the conventional criteria, however, will note that the details of the calculation methods were included in the last section. This is because the calculation of the growth rate of the portfolio value is an intermediate step in the calculation of the real growth rate. In the same way the calculation of the return on investment is an intermediate step in the calculation of the real return.

Having calculated the trend in the rate of growth, it is seen from the example in Table 6.3 that there has been a deterioration in recent years, the Growths/a being 5.4 per cent, 3.6 per cent and −11.8 per cent respectively over three, two and one year(s). These figures in themselves are not very informative, however. As was the case for individual shares, it is important to know whether the growth rate of the portfolio was greater or less than would have been expected if the shares in the portfolio had tracked the All Share Index. It is also important to know whether there has been a real growth in the value of the portfolio. To answer these questions the real growth rate of the portfolio is calculated, together with the target growth rate. The relationship between the growth rate and the real growth rate was recorded in the Definitions appended to Table 5.5, the growth rate in that case referring to the share price. The same equation can be used for portfolio value, if the portfolio growth rate (Port gr) is substituted in the equation for the share price growth rate, i.e.:

$$\% \text{ Real growth} = 100 \times (\text{Port gr} - \text{Infl})/(100 + \text{Infl})$$

The rate of inflation (Infl) is synonymous with the % RPI growth. The *target growth* can be calculated by substituting in the above equation the All Share Index growth for the portfolio growth rate, (see example in Table 6.4).

The yield (net) of the portfolio, in any one year, is calculated by adding together the dividends paid on each of the share holdings and dividing by the value of all the shares in the portfolio, averaged over the year. The *target yield* is the yield achieved by the All Share Index.

The performance of the portfolio, as indicated by the growth figures calculated in Table 6.3, over the review period, is seen to be misleading when the results are compared with those analysed in terms of the *real growth* and *target growth* and shown in Table 6.4. There is, in fact, a negative *real growth* over the three years, and the

Table 6.4 Portfolios – real and target growth rates

Year end		1987	1988	1989	1990
Investment,£				300	
Inv frac				205	
Port value,£		1000	1100	1700	1500
Trial value,£	Gr	1000	1054	1422	1499
Trial value,£	Gr			1700	1499
%Growth/a to end 1990					
Port value		5.4	3.6	−11.8	
Real		−2.4	−4.5	−19.3	
Target		−2.6	−2.4	−21.1	
%Yield(net)		3.0	3.6	3.1	3.8
%Targ yield		3.1	3.2	3.2	4.1
RPI		103.3	110.6	119.1	130.1
AlShI		891	926	1205	1038
%Growth/a to end 1990					
RPI		8.0	8.5	9.2	
AlShI		5.2	5.9	−13.8	

Definitions:

a) See definitions appended to Tables 6.2 and 6.3 for Port growth calculations.

b) See Tables 5.5 and 5.6 definitions for RPI and AlShI rates of growth.

c) % Real growth = 100×(Port growth−Infl)/(100 + Infl)

d) % Targ growth = 100×(AlShI growth − Infl)/(100 + Infl)

performance is even worse over two and one year(s). Nevertheless the portfolio performance over the three years was slightly better than the market as a whole, i.e. the *real growth* was −2.4 per cent per annum compared with a *target growth* of −2.6 per cent per annum. The *target growth* figures reflect the fact that the period 1988 to 1990 was a poor time to be investing in ordinary shares. Over the last two years and one year the *real growth* was increasingly negative, i.e. there was an increasing loss in the real value of the portfolio. Comparing the *real growth* with the *target growth*, however, indicates that this was largely a reflection of the performance of the whole market. The portfolio yield was close to the *target yield* through the review period.

As was the case for the share price analysis outlined in Chapter 5, the assessment of the performance of the portfolio is best carried out for the different categories of portfolio first, before carrying it out for the whole portfolio (providing the size of the category portfolios is large enough to make the results meaningful). A full assessment of the performance of the investments also requires a knowledge of the yield for each category, of course.

The method outlined in Chapter 5 for calculating the growth of individual shares can now be seen to be essentially the same as the method just described for measuring the performance of portfolios. In the former case the portfolio consists of one particular share so that the portfolio value on any date is the market price of the share on that date; the 'invested' figure is zero throughout. The only difference is that the calculation of the rate of growth of the portfolio, over more than one year, is more complicated than the calculation for an individual share. The T&E method is needed for a portfolio whereas the calculation for the single share can be accomplished using either the @RATE function (LOTUS software) or compound interest tables.

The comparative advantages and disadvantages of expressing the performance of an individual share in terms of the *real return*, as well as the *real growth* and yield (see Chapter 5), apply equally well to portfolio performance. The recommended System therefore includes the calculation and recording of both the *real growth* and yield, and also the *real return* for the assessment of portfolio performance. The calculation of the *real return* by the direct method, using the IRR (internal rate of return) function, is outlined in the next section. (It is assumed that a function for this calculation is available in the investor's spreadsheet program).

THE REAL RETURN OF A PORTFOLIO

The measurement of total return takes into account the benefits from both the capital (i.e. share price or portfolio value) growth and the net dividends. By using this concept the performance of an investment can be expressed in terms of a single variable, the *real return*, rather than two variables, the *real growth* and the net yield. A better understanding of the meaning of the rate of return of a portfolio can be obtained by regarding it as the highest rate of interest that could be paid, without losing money, on a loan raised to finance the investment in the portfolio. The money can be repaid at any time, with the net dividends for instance, or reinvested to earn the same rate of interest as the loan. It follows from this definition that the *real return* is equal to the *real growth* in the portfolio value, when the net dividends are reinvested.

As was the case for the growth rate of a share or portfolio, the return/a could be used as one of the principal criteria of share or portfolio performance. It is the conventional criterion for financial performance, and the arguments in its favour are the same as those summarised in the last section. Even stronger arguments, however, favour the use of the return corrected for the effects of inflation, i.e. the *real return/a*, for the System. As was the case for the growth rate figures, the calculation of the *return/a* is an intermediate step in the calculation of the *real return/a*. Those investors who decide to stay with the conventional criteria can therefore find the calculation methods they need described in detail in this section.

The direct method chosen for measuring the *real return* of a portfolio is the IRR method. IRR is the name of the function in the Lotus spreadsheet for calculating the internal rate of return of a range of cash flows. The fact that there is a function for this calculation in many of the computer programmes available to private investors, means that the calculations can be carried out quite quickly. The IRR method can only deal with cash flows at regular intervals, however. In contrast to the T&E method for determining the growth rate of portfolios, therefore, where the actual date of an investment enters into the calculation, the net investment in each period must be used in the IRR method of calculating the *real return*. The potential inaccuracies in this method are discussed in more detail in Appendix 5.

Most private investors will find that the IRR method of calculation is of sufficient accuracy when measuring the *real return* over periods greater than a year, providing the data entry intervals are quarterly or less.

An alternative method for calculating the rate of return of a portfolio is the discounted cash flow (DCF) method. DCF is a method commonly used for measuring the return on investment for capital projects in industry and commerce. In principle this is similar to the T&E method described earlier in this chapter, except that the net dividends are included in the calculation. It has the advantage of taking account of the date of investment and the disadvantage of requiring a trial and error type calculation. To take account of the date of payment of dividends, in the same way as was used for investments, would add significantly to the work required of the investor. The DCF method, as just outlined, was therefore rejected in favour of the IRR method. Incidentally, the DCF method most commonly used in business makes use of regular time intervals, and is virtually the same as the method defined in the System as the IRR method.

Some examples of using the IRR function are shown in Table 6.5. The cash flow at the beginning of the review period is the value of the portfolio (as if it had been purchased), and is negative. The net-of-tax dividends are positive cash flows whilst the net (i.e. purchases minus sales) investments are negative cash flows. The cash flow for the last

Table 6.5 Example of the IRR calculation

	Cash flow					
	£ End '85	£ End '86	£ End '87	£ End '88	£ End '89	%Return p.a.over 4 Years
Capital	−1000	−1000	0	0	2795	
Net divi	0	100	210	231	254	
Cash flow	−1000	−900	210	231	3049	**20.0**

Definitions and assumptions:

a) Investments are made at the year-end, before the portfolio is valued. The value of the portfolio at the end of 1985 is £1,000, whilst a further £1,000 is invested in the portfolio at the end of 1986.

b) Dividends are paid at the year-end, before the portfolio is valued.

c) The rate of return is calculated using the Lotus 'Internal Rate of Return', i.e. the @IRR function. For instance, for the range of values of cash flow shown in the last line of the Table:

% return/a = @IRR(Guess return,Range) = 20 per cent per annum

where the Range is the range of figures in the line starting with −1,000 and finishing with 3,049.

period of the review is equal to the value of the portfolio (as if it had been sold), plus the net dividends and minus the net investment in the last period.

In Table 6.6 the IRR method is used to calculate the *real return* of the same portfolio as that used in the example in Table 6.4.

The cash flow figures are those for the full period of the review. The next three lines CashFl, (IRR) form the ranges for the calculation of the IRR rate of return for the three years, two years and one year respectively, ending 1990.

For example, for the three years to end 1990:

$$\% \ \text{Return/a} = @\text{IRR}(\text{Guess rate,Range})$$
$$= @\text{IRR}(10\ \%,-1000 \ . \ . \ 1556)$$
$$= 10 \ \text{per cent per annum}$$

The 10 per cent figure is value copied to the next row, i.e. to the %Return /a row.

In order to calculate the %Return/a for the two years from end 1988 to end 1990, the portfolio value at the end of 1988, £1,100, is entered in the 1988 column of the second CashFl,(IRR) row. The equation now becomes:

$$\% \ \text{Return/a} = @\text{IRR}(\text{Guess rate,Range})$$
$$= @\text{IRR}(10\ \%,-1100 \ . \ . \ 1556)$$
$$= 8.2 \ \text{per cent per annum}$$

To calculate the %Return/a for the year from end 1989 to end 1990, the portfolio value at the end of 1989, £1,700, is entered in the 1989 column of the third CashFl,(IRR) row. The equation now becomes:

$$\% \ \text{Return/a} = @\text{IRR}(\text{Guess rate,Range})$$
$$= @\text{IRR}(10\ \%,-1700 \ . \ . \ 1556)$$
$$= -8.5 \ \text{per cent per annum}$$

The *target return* is calculated in the same way as it was for individual shares, and indeed produces the very same figures over the same time periods.

$$\% \ \text{Targ return/a} = \% \ \text{Targ growth/a} + \text{average} \ \% \ \text{Targ yield(net)}$$

In practice, in order to conserve space and make the tables more

Table 6.6 Portfolios – the rate of return (IRR method)

Year end	1987	1988	1989	1990
Investment,£			300	
Divi(net),£	30	40	53	56
Port value,£	1000	1100	1700	1500
Cash flow, £	−1000	40	−247	1556
Cash Fl,(IRR),£	−1000	40	−247	1556
		−1100	−247	1556
			−247	1556
			−1700	1556
% IRR				
Period to end 1990				
% Return/a	10.0	8.2	−8.5	
% Real return/a	**1.9**	**−0.2**	**−16.2**	
% Targ return/a	**0.9**	**1.1**	**−17.4**	
% Yield(net)	3.0	3.6	3.1	3.8
% Targ yield	3.1	3.2	3.2	4.1
RPI	103.3	110.6	119.1	130.1
AlShI	891	926	1205	1038
Period to end 1990				
% Infl.	8.0	8.5	9.2	
% AlShI growth	5.2	5.9	−13.8	
% Targ growth	−2.6	−2.4	−21.1	

easily read, only one row in the spreadsheet is allocated to CashFl,IRR. As the starting date moves towards the end date, so the CashFl,IRR on the starting date is altered to equal the portfolio value.

At first sight the rows % IRR and % Return duplicate each other. It will be found, however, that the % IRR figures for the longer review periods will change as the % IRR for the shorter periods are calculated. It is for this reason that, after each % IRR is calculated, it is value copied to the % Return row.

CHOICE OF METHODS

The direct method recommended for measuring the *real growth* of a portfolio was outlined earlier in the chapter and is called the T&E

method. The method uses a trial and error calculation and can accommodate major investments at irregular intervals.

The direct method recommended for measuring the *real return* of a portfolio was described in the last section, and makes use of the IRR function in the Lotus spreadsheet. It analyses the cash flow of the portfolio and to achieve this requires the investments and dividends to be allocated to regular periods of time, such as quarters of a year.

The third important performance assessment criterion is the yield. For portfolios the net yield should be calculated by dividing the total net dividend over the past year by the average portfolio value, rather than by the portfolio value on the end date of the year over which the *real return* is being calculated, as is usual for an individual share. This modification is more accurate in fundamental terms (see Appendix 2), but is also necessary because of the effect major purchases or sales can have on the value of the portfolio on a single date.

The stage has now been reached where three variables have been defined which are central to the measurement of the performance of a portfolio. The means for calculating the variables have also been described in detail. The three variables are:

%Dividend yield (net).

%*Real growth* per annum, T&E method.

%*Real return* per annum, IRR method.

These three variables are not, however, independent of each other. For instance, it is shown in Appendix 4 that the three variables can be related with reasonable accuracy by the equation:

$$\%\,\text{Real return/a} = \%\,\text{Real growth/a} + \%\,\text{Yield (net)}$$

It is therefore possible to calculate the *real return* of a portfolio in two different ways, either by the direct method, from the cash flows using the IRR function, or by the indirect method, from the *real growth* and the yield. The former is described as the *real return* (IRR) and the latter as the *real return* (T&E). The situation can be summarised as follows:

Variable	Calculated from
Option 1	
Real growth (T&E)	Portfolio values and investments
Real return (T&E)	Real growth (T&E) and yield
Option 2	
Real return (IRR)	Cash flows in/out of portfolio
Real growth (IRR)	Real return (IRR) and yield

The equation used to calculate the *real growth* (IRR) is as follows:

$$\% \, \text{Real growth} = \% \, \text{Real return} - \% \, \text{average yield (net)}$$

The choice of Option 1 or Option 2 is left to the investor. Some investors will choose to use both options, perhaps over different time periods. For the majority of investors, who will want to choose one or other of the options, the relative advantages and disadvantages are shown below:

Option 1 based on *real growth* by the T&E method:

Advantages:
- Acceptable degree of accuracy
  It is not necessary to value portfolio at least quarterly

Disadvantages:
- Drafting of equations is more time-consuming

Option 2 based on *real return* by IRR method:

Advantages:
- Do not need to draft many equations and therefore easier and quicker to use
- It is not necessary to calculate the invested fraction

Disadvantages:
- Need to record data on at least a quarterly basis to achieve an acceptable degree of accuracy

The *real returns* for the portfolio used in the examples in Tables 6.4

and 6.6, together with the *target returns*, are shown in Table 6.7, calculated by the two different methods. The *target returns* are the same, whichever method is used to arrive at the *real return*. The *real returns* (IRR) are values copied directly from Table 6.6, whilst the *real returns* (T&E) are calculated from the *real growths* and yields, which in turn were value copied from Table 6.4.

Table 6.7 Comparison of the IRR and T&E methods

	Year end	*1987*	*1988*	*1989*	*1990*
Periods to end 1990					
%Real return/a					
IRR method		1.9	−0.2	−16.2	
T&E method		1.1	−1.1	−15.5	
%Targ return/a					
Both methods		0.9	1.2	−17.2	
% Real growth/a		−2.4	−4.5	−19.3	
T&E method					
%Yield(net)		3.0	3.6	3.1	3.8

The results are reasonably close in view of the fact that the assumptions about the dates of the investment and the dividends were different in the two calculations.

The *real returns* for the selected portfolio, together with the *target returns*, are shown in Table 6.8, calculated by the two different methods.

Table 6.8 Comparison for the selected portfolio

	Year end	*1988*	*1989*	*1990*	*1991*
Periods to 30/12/92					
%Real return/a					
IRR method		5.8	1.3	15.0	22.9
T&E method		5.7	1.8	14.6	22.1
%Targ return/a					
Both methods		7.5	2.6	14.3	18.0

The results are seen to be sufficiently close for most private investors. It must, however, be recognised that the amounts invested were relatively small, so that the fact that the IRR method was calculated with yearly intervals, rather than the recommended quarterly intervals, did not result in an important error.

In conclusion, the System of performance measurement recommended in this book requires the monitoring of the yield, the *real growth* and the *real return* of the portfolio, together with the corresponding targets. Whether these criteria are calculated by Option 1, as described above, based on the T&E method, or Option 2, based on the IRR method, is left for the individual investor to choose. The results of applying these methods to the *selected portfolio* are shown in Table 13.4. The relative accuracies of the two options are discussed in more detail in Appendix 4.

7

PEP PERFORMANCE

' "It was as true as taxes is," said Mr. Barkis. "And nothing's truer than them." '
Charles Dickens, 1812–1870

Each Pep is analysed by using the method developed for portfolios, so that annual investments in the same Pep can be taken into account. It is not really practical to analyse the Peps as one category of the whole portfolio, since it is difficult to get common valuation dates for the shares and the Peps. This is because the dates chosen by the managers to value the Peps are often not the same as the data input dates chosen by the investor for the shares in the portfolio. Furthermore, different Peps often have different valuation dates. The performance of the Peps are best assessed separately, therefore, as demonstrated overleaf, in Table 7.1, for the Save and Prosper Managed Portfolio Pep, with dividends reinvested. The trial values were erased after they had served their purpose in the calculation of the growth rates.

The *real return* of the S & P Pep over the full period of the review, at 6.2 per cent per annum, compares with the approximately 4 per cent that could have been obtained over the same period in a savings account. The *real return* is also significantly higher than the *target return* (6.2 per cent compared with 2.7 per cent). It should also be noted that although the performance in real terms deteriorated somewhat over the last year, it improved appreciably when compared with the *target return*, partly because the more recent results are not affected by the costs associated with the purchase of the Pep. The

Table 7.1 Pep performance

	31/12/87	31/12/88	05/04/90	05/04/91	03/04/92
Years to 3/4/92	4.3	3.3	2.0	1.0	
Invested,£	2000	3000			
Pep value,£	1870	4936	6163	7373	7926
%Real return/a to 3/4/92					
Pep	**6.2**	**8.4**	**7.9**	**3.3**	
Target	**2.8**	**3.6**	**0.5**	**−7.0**	
RPI	103	111	124	132	137
AlShI	891	926	1102	1232	1142
Targ yield,%	4.2	4.6	4.9	4.6	5.2
% Growth/a to 3/4/92					
Pep value	13.5	15.8	13.4	7.5	
RPI (Inflation)	6.9	6.8	5.1	4.0	
AlShI	6.0	6.7	1.8	−7.3	

Notes:

1 Both the £2,000 and the £3,000 investments were made at the end of the year, so that there is no need to calculate the *invested fraction*.

2 The Growth between 31/12/88 and 5/4/90 has been calculated by multiplying the %Growth by 15/12 (the ratio of the months between these dates to the months in a year). This is considered a good enough approximation for the purpose. It is necessary because S & P changed their valuation dates.

3 When assessing the performance of this Pep, allowance has to be made for the fact that the gross dividends have been reinvested; i.e. the yield is nil. The *%Real return* has been chosen as the criteria best suited to the assessment of Pep performance, therefore:

%Real return = %Real growth in this case

The *real growth* figures were calculated using the T&E method.

overall performance can be described as satisfactory and improving.

Many Peps will have been established with a single lump-sum investment and have received no further injection of funds. The performance of such Peps can be analysed more simply by using the methods developed for individual shares (see Chapter 5). An example is given in Appendix 6.

8

THE COMPUTER AND THE SOFTWARE

'But the age of chivalry is gone. That of sophisters, economists, and calculators, has succeeded; and the glory of Europe is extinguished forever.'
Edmund Burke, 1729–1797

The System of performance analysis outlined in this book could perhaps be applied to a handful of shareholdings without requiring the use of a computer, but the work would be laborious. The author has developed the System using a computer with the following specification:

Amstrad PC2086/30
IBM compatible PC
Memory size-RAM: 640 Kilobytes
CPU: 8MHz 8086 processor
Floppy disk: 1 × 3.5″, 720K
Hard disk: 1 × 32MB
Operating System: MS-DOS 3.30
Software: Lotus Symphony 2.0

The RAM memory limits the number of share-holdings that can be analysed to about 30 in the files as described, although this number could be increased if the length of the review period and/or the frequency of data input was reduced. A considerable increase in the number of share-holdings to be analysed can be achieved simply by increasing the number of files. The data for the *selected portfolio* has been processed in three files, which are described in Chapter 9.

Faster computers with much bigger RAMs are now available at the same cost as the one described, which was purchased in 1990. With such computers all the data can be analysed in a single file, thereby eliminating the time taken to transfer data between files. Each of the files described in the next chapter then becomes simply a table of data in a single file. In the case of the *selected portfolio*, the three tables would be arranged one below the other. Table 13.2 could, for instance, occupy lines 1 to 99, Table 13.3 lines 100 to 199 and Table 13.4 lines 200 to 299. On the other hand, it is sometimes advantageous to have each table in a separate file. For instance, it allows different columns to be hidden in each table. Modern spreadsheets offer more flexibility than Lotus Symphony, particularly when combined with Windows. With this type of software the comments above are no longer relevant.

To summarise, the bigger memory gives the investor the freedom to choose whether to put a number of tables in the same file.

Readers with Lotus 123 can retrieve the MspData File, for instance, from the floppy disk by inserting the disk into the computer (assumed to be drive A), selecting FILE and then RETRIEVE, and typing 'A:/MSPDATA.WR1'. The file can then be saved using the appropriate extension, probably WK3.

Readers with Microsoft Excel should select FILE OPEN and then select Lotus Files (✱.WR1.) from the List Files of Type drop-down list.

9

THE FILES AND THE FREQUENCY OF DATA INPUT

'There are few ways in which a man can be more innocently employed than in getting money.'
Samuel Johnson, 1775.

The files have been designed so that each has a particular purpose and also so that it is seldom necessary to transfer data from one file to another. The first file contains the basic information on all the investments. The second and third files contain the calculations of the performance criteria, the second for the equity shares and the third for the portfolio. The fourth file contains the performance calculations for the fixed interest investments. The files, their contents and the chapter and/or appendix in which their constructions are described are listed below. The use of the files for the *selected portfolio* can be seen in Tables 13.2 to 13.4. (There is also a file MspMktSt, which contains the market statistics – see Chapter 10.)

MEASURING SHARE PERFORMANCE: DATA (MspData)

Chapter 6, Appendix 1 and for *selected portfolio*, Table 13.2

The first file (*MspData*) contains information about each of the investments held, including the identification numbers on the certificates and the price of the shares on 31 March 1982 (the date from which capital gains are calculated) or on the date of purchase, whichever was the later. The shares are listed in category order. In the case of the *selected portfolio* the order is as follows:

Type	Owner
Ordinary	DM
Ordinary	MM
Unit trusts	DM
Unit trusts	MM
Unit trusts(accumulative)	DM
Unit trusts(accumulative)	MM

Mid-market prices are used for ordinary shares and bid prices for unit trusts. This should be borne in mind if the 31 March 1982 prices are going to be used to calculate capital gains tax. The purchase costs shown are the gross costs, whilst the money recorded as being received on sale is the net amount. Purchases and sales are recorded, thereby allowing the calculation of the net investment in each year or quarter; the *invested fraction* is also calculated for each year (see Chapter 6). The invested figure recorded on 31 March 1982, the start of the review period, is the value of the shares held on that day.

MEASURING SHARE PERFORMANCE: PRICES (MspPri)

Chapter 5, Appendix 1 and for *selected portfolio*, Table 13.3

The second and third files have the purpose of recording the information and calculating the criteria needed to assess the performance of the equity investments. The shares are divided into the same categories as for the first file. The second file (*MspPri*) contains information on the original number of shares in the holding plus any additional scrip issue shares and the price per share, over the period of the review. These figures allow the *corrected price* to be calculated (see Chapter 5) and hence the *P/A ratio* for each holding. The *real gain* is calculated to allow the potential liability to CGT to be monitored. An actual charge will only arise, of course, if the shares are sold and also if the gain is greater than the exemption limit (£5,800 per person in 1992/93).

The *real growth/a* and *target growth/a* are calculated which, together with the gross yield and price/earnings ratio, as reported in the press, allow the performance of each share holding to be assessed. The *real return* for each share is then calculated. The averages of the *real return* figures can also be calculated for the whole portfolio.

MEASURING SHARE PERFORMANCE: PORTFOLIO (MspPort)

Chapter 6, Appendices 1 and 4, and for *selected portfolio*, Table 13.4.

The third file (*MspPort*) contains, for each holding, the following data: total number of shares, price/share, dividends/share, dividends paid, net dividend yield and value of shares in holding. The net dividend yield is calculated from the dividends paid and the share price rather than being calculated from the data in the newspapers. The shares are divided into the same categories as for the first and second files. The dividend yield (net) and the value are calculated for each share holding and for the total portfolio. The figures for the net invested and the *invested fraction* are transferred to this file from the 'MspData' file. The *real growth* and *real return* figures, together with the corresponding target figures, are then calculated for the portfolio(s).

MEASURING SHARE PERFORMANCE: F.I. INVESTMENTS (MspFIInv)

Chapter 12, Appendix 1

The last file, (*MspFIInv*) is the only file containing information on the performance of the fixed interest investments in the portfolio. It contains a record, over a period of say seven years, of the number of stock units held, the stock price, the dividends paid and the market value. The performance of the investments is also assessed, using the *real return* as the key criterion. The *target return* and the *real return* on the three-month inter-bank rate are calculated for comparison (see Table 13.1). Since it is very unlikely that capital gains tax will have to be paid on the disposal of any fixed interest investments, there is not the same motivation to start the review period on 31 March 1982, as was the case for equities. The investor will probably choose to start the review on the date of purchase or the date on which stock prices first start to be collected. It will be remembered that details of the type and specifications of the investments, their purchase and sale (where applicable), and data from the certificates are held in the *MspData* file.

THE FREQUENCY OF DATA INPUT

The data recorded on the computer is of two types, that of a permanent nature relating to the shares held, such as category of investment, dates dividends paid, identification numbers on certificates, etc., and the other type concerned with share prices, yields etc. The latter is the type under discussion in this section.

Share prices fall, other things being equal, from the date they go 'ex-div', since a purchaser of the shares after that date does not have the right to the latest dividend. The effect on the share price is very small in comparison with the other reasons for variation, since dividends nowadays are almost always paid twice per year and average less than 2 per cent on each occasion. In order to retain simplicity in the System, this source of variation is not subject to routine analysis. It should not be overlooked, however, in cases where the reader is looking for a reason for small changes in the price of a particular share. When share prices on the same date each year are being compared, there is normally no 'ex-div' effect.

Investors who do not have, and cannot get, information on share prices going back over the years, should start collecting share prices now, so that they can start to analyse their investment performance and review their policy as soon as possible. The best time to start is, of course, the day the first investment is made. For those investors who have held some shares since 31 March 1982, even though they do not have any share prices in the intervening period, this should be the starting date for the review. This allows the investors to review regularly their potential liability to CGT, since shares purchased before 31 March 1982 are valued as if they had been purchased on that day. (The prices on 31 March 1982 can be obtained from the *Financial Times* publication on capital gains tax.)

It is suggested that the frequency with which data is retained is four times per year between the date of purchase of the first shareholding (or 31 March 1982 if this is later) and 1990 or 1991. This might seem rather infrequent in view of the large swings that can take place in share prices. For the great majority of shares, however, although the variable being monitored, e.g. the *real growth*, will change considerably during periods such as the 1987 stock market crash, the corresponding target, in this case the *target growth*, will change to the same extent.

The end of the tax year, i.e. 5 April, is a suitable date for recording data, since annual dividends and capital gains up to that date have to be reported to the Inland Revenue. Another obvious date for entering data is the last day in the calendar year on which trading on the floor of the Stock Exchange takes place. The other two recommended recording dates in each year, up to 1990 or 1991, are therefore the ends of June and September.

Data should be entered more frequently over the latest two or three years, for the short-term review, which monitors the *real gain*,£, yield and P/E ratio. The *P/A ratio* (i.e. the ratio 'Price / AlShI' rebased to 1.0) of most shares will change by small amounts, if at all, even during periods when the market is moving rapidly. The reason is that professional investors are always on the look-out to buy shares whose prices have fallen behind the market for reasons unrelated to company performance. The private investor is looking for an early warning of a share which is beginning to move against the trend; i.e. he is looking for an unusual change in the *P/A ratio*. Some investors might, therefore, enter the prices of particular shares as frequently as daily. As time passes much of this data can be erased, so that only quarterly figures are retained.

Recommendations have been made in this section on the

frequency with which data should be entered and retained. It is emphasised, however, that this is very much a matter for individual choice by the investor. The frequency of monitoring of the *real growth* and the *real return* would be expected to fall in the range monthly to annually, whilst monitoring of the short-term variables such as *P/A ratio* would be expected to take place at least monthly.

The availability of space prevents the use of the optimum frequency of data input in the tables printed in this book. This means that some of the tables do not give the full picture of share or portfolio performance, but only enough to demonstrate the application of the System.

10

INVESTMENT AND MARKET STATISTICS

'In civil business; what first? Boldness; What second, and third? Boldness. And yet boldness is a child of ignorance and baseness.'
Francis Bacon, 1561–1626

Before going on to discuss the performance of the *selected portfolio* in Chapter 11, it is important to be able to set this performance off against the background of the performance of the economy and the market as a whole. This chapter is included for this purpose. The relevant figures are shown in Table 13.1 (File MSpMktSt).

EFFECT OF COMPANY SIZE ON INDICES

An understanding of the reasons for the movement in the prices of individual shares is helped by first of all understanding the reasons for the relative movement of the different share price indices. An inspection of the figures in Table 13.1 will help. Details of the way these indices are calculated can be obtained from the *Financial Times* publication *A Guide to Financial Times Statistics*. The ratios of some of the indices (rebased to 1.0 on 31 March 1982) show how they have moved relative to one another.

The 30 Share (ordinary), 100 Share (Footsie) and All Share *Financial Times* indices recorded in Table 13.1 indicate that share prices rose rapidly between 1982 and 1984, and then steadily until the quite steep fall in 1990. The fall was short-lived, however, the recovery starting early in 1991. (Because of the shortage of space, these figures can only give a broad indication of the pattern of change in share prices. The severe fall in prices in November 1987, for instance, is not shown). The All Share Index nearly quadrupled its value over the seven plus years between 31 March 1982 and the end of 1989. It was towards the end of 1992 before the high levels of the All Share Index experienced in the late 1980s were exceeded regularly. The All Share Index continued rising through 1993.

The companies in the 30 share and 100 share indices are the larger companies in the UK (sometimes referred to as the 'Blue Chip' companies). The All Share Index, on the other hand, contains many small and medium sized companies. The new 250 share index has only been introduced recently; in a year or two its movement relative to the other indices will be worth monitoring. Looking at the ratios 'AlShI/30Share' and 'AlShI/100Share' recorded in Table 13.1 leads to the conclusion that the smaller companies performed better than the larger ones between 1982 and 1987. The position then reversed, particularly when the 1990 recession struck and smaller companies started going bankrupt in increasing numbers. Over the almost 11 years of the review period ending on 30 December 1992, however, some of the advantages of the smaller companies have remained, the All Share Index out-performing the 30 Share and the 100 Share Indices by 9 per cent and 8 per cent respectively. It is worth noting that the 30 Share Index, because of the way in which it is constructed, is only useful for monitoring short-term changes in the mood of the market. It is not suitable for use as a standard, for comparing with the performance of either a single share or a portfolio, over the medium or longer term.

YIELDS AND GROWTH RATES

In Table 13.1 the performance of the All Share Index in real terms is reviewed by calculating the ratio 'AlShI/RPI' and also by calculating the target growth rate. The rate of inflation is calculated from the RPI figures. It can be argued that the underlying rate of inflation, which excludes house mortgage interest from the calculation, is more relevant to investment monitoring than the RPI. Despite this argument the System has used the RPI as an indication of inflation because it is easily available and commonly used.

It will be remembered that the *target growth* is the *real growth* that would have been achieved if the share(s) had tracked the All Share Index. The *target growth* therefore measures the real growth in the All Share Index. The % inflation/a and the *targ growth/a* are calculated for the previous year and also from the date at the top of the column to the end of the review period.

The ratio 'AlShI/RPI' shows an increase, over the full review period, from 1.00 to 2.44. The *target growth* was very good in 1982/84, 1985 and 1986 at 18.7, 9.5 and 17.6 per cent per annum respectively. It fell away in 1987 and 1988 but recovered strongly in 1989 to 20.8 per cent. All of the growth in 1989 was lost in 1990. Each of the next two years saw an increasing rate of growth, the *target growth* reaching 14.9 per cent per annum in 1992. Over the whole review period to 30 December 1992 the *target growth* achieved a figure of 8.6 per cent per annum, a satisfactory performance. However, if the *target growth* is measured from 29 December 1984 to the end of the review period, it was only 5.3 per cent per annum, whilst from 29 December 1989 it was −1.1 per cent per annum.

RETURN ON INVESTMENT

The total return on investment (see Chapter 5) takes into account both the growth in the capital value, and the net income received. The System defines the *real return* of a share as the addition of the *real growth* and the average yield (net). This is a simplification of the true relationship between these variables, but is sufficiently accurate for most purposes, as demonstrated in Appendix 4. When the performance of shares tracks the All Share Index, the *real growth* is termed the *target growth*, the *real return* the *target return* and the yield the target yield. These targets, which are calculated/recorded in Table 13.1, are essentially measurements of the performance of the All Share Index.

The dividend yields for the shares included in the All Share Index, i.e. the *target yields*, are recorded in Table 13.1, as also is the three-month inter-bank rate of interest. The latter is the average of the rate of interest paid by borrowers or received by lenders, for transactions with a three month term, between institutions such as the banks, for large sums of money. The three-month inter-bank interest rate is quoted to give an indication of the rates that can be earned by bank or building society savings accounts: £5,000, for instance, would earn gross interest, in an instant access account in March, 1992, of about 2 per cent below the inter-bank rate. By October 1993 interest rates had fallen and the difference had fallen to about 1 per cent. As the amount deposited and the notice of withdrawal increases, the rate of interest approaches closer to the inter-bank rate. The *target returns* for the shares and the *real returns* of the bank account are calculated from a range of dates, over the past year and over the years to the end of the review period. These figures allow a comparison to be made between the performance of the average share, as represented by the All Share Index, and a bank deposit account.

It should be noted that the figures in Table 13.1 are biased in favour of the shares, in that no account is taken of transaction costs. The bias is relatively unimportant over the longer periods of review. On the other hand, the private investor would normally not receive interest rates from the bank or building society as high as the inter-bank rate.

Inspection of the results in Table 13.1 and Figures 10.1 and 10.2 allow a comparison to be made between the performance of the shares and the bank savings account. The inter-bank rate of interest has run at between two and three times the gross dividend yield on equities over the last 10 years or so. The apparently superior performance of the bank deposit is soon reversed, however, when the effect of inflation is taken into account. It is seen from Table 13.1 and Figure 10.1 that, over any one year, the *real return* of the shares is only lower than that of the bank account on two occasions out of eight. It is also apparent that the performance of the shares was appreciably and consistently better than the bank savings up to and including 1987, but not thereafter. Looking at the results for various periods up to the end of the review period, i.e. 30 December 1992, (Figure 10.2), it is seen that the *real return* of the shares is only once

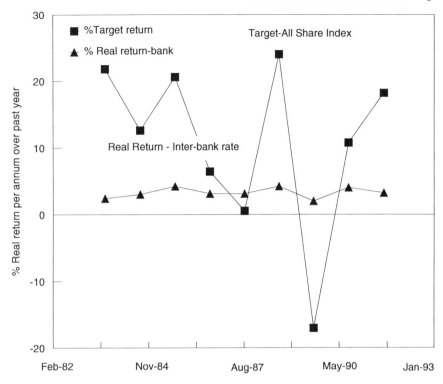

Figure 10.1   Shares and bank accounts: % real return over past year

lower than that of the bank account. Over the full period of the review the average share gave a *target return* of 12 per cent per annum compared with the 3 per cent per annum achieved by the bank. It is apparent that the performance measured over the various periods up to the end date is more informative than the performance measured over the past year.

Since mid-1993 the *Financial Times* has been reporting the total return on the various share indices. The figures are calculated without any allowance for tax on the dividends, having been designed mainly for use by insurance companies, etc.

In summary, the *real return* on the shares is more variable than that on the bank account. Even when both capital appreciation and net interest are taken into account, there are periods when the shares have lost real value, which is not the case for the bank account. If

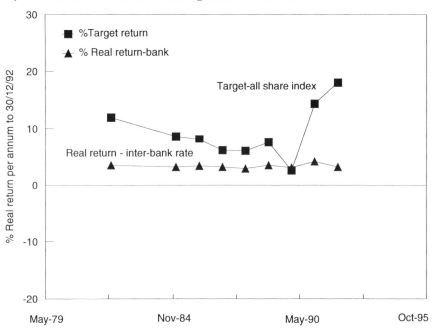

Figure 10.2   Shares and bank accounts: % real return over periods to 30/12/92

space had allowed the data to be entered more frequently, this difference would have been even more apparent. These figures reinforce the precept that investors should not buy shares with money that might be needed, at short notice, at some unknown date in the future. Over longer periods of time, however, and with good timing, shares are a much better investment than a bank or building society savings account.

11

HOW THE SELECTED PORTFOLIO PERFORMED

'Business was his pleasure; pleasure was his business.'
John Dyer, early 18th century

DESCRIPTION OF SHARES AND SOURCES OF DATA

A portfolio of equity shares has been constructed, comprising eight ordinaries, three unit trusts and two unit trusts (acc). Two of the share holdings are in the same company (ICI), but with different owners initially. Each share in the portfolio has been chosen to demonstrate a different feature, as summarised below, and some information about the companies whose shares/units are in the portfolio is included in the summary.

Notes on shares in selected portfolio

Commercial Union

Composite insurance company.

Dividend (£165) reinvested in 1987 to purchase 55 shares. Total holding sold in 1989 to M&G and 1,090 M&G Recovery Unit Trust units received in exchange; hence no selling or buying costs, other than the 5 per cent difference between the bid and offer prices.

Davis Services (previously Godfrey Davis)

Operates textile maintenance, vehicle supply and services (now dis-continued), and site services businesses.

Shares received in exchange for Sunlight Services shares when Godfrey Davis (now called Davis Services) took over that company in 1987. Treated as a simultaneous sale and purchase, the price being the cash offer alternative.

ICI

Major international chemicals producer.

Ordinary shares in ICI held in 1982 by both owner D and owner M. Shares owned by D transfered to M (see note following this section for procedure needed to accomplish this without incurring costs), when separate taxation introduced for husband and wife. Valued at mid-market price on day of transfer. Demerger took place in June, 1993, when shareholders were given one share in the new company, Zeneca, for each ICI share held. The bioscience businesses, such as pharmaceuticals, were transferred into Zeneca.

Marks and Spencer

Major retail store company.

Scrip issue (1 for 1) increased number of shares in holding from 600 to 1,200 in 1984. Dividend (£23.45) reinvested to purchase 10 shares in 1991.

Sunlight Services

Operated laundries and linen supplies.

Taken over by Godfrey Davis, now Davis Services (see entry for Davis Services).

Whitbread

Businesses in beer, pubs and chain leisure retailing.

No change in holding during period of review.

BAA

Operates airports.

Privatisation issue explains small holding. Payment for shares phased in two stages. 10 per cent bonus issue after three years.

Henderson Income & Growth Unit Trust

Unit trust invested in UK mainly, aimed at increasing income combined with prospects for capital growth.

No change in holding during period of review.

Invesco Great British Companies Unit Trust

Formerly MIM Britania Great British Companies, prior to that County Bank Growth Investment UT, National Westminster Growth Investment UT and Westminster Hambro Growth Investment UT. Invested in leading UK companies, aimed at increasing income and long term capital growth.

A 10–1 sub-division of units took place in 1989.

S&P Investment Trust Unit Trust

Invested worldwide in investment trusts.

No change in holding during period of review.

M&G Compound Growth Fund Unit Trust

Invested principally in UK. Aim is capital growth.

All income reinvested, i.e. accumulation units.

M&G Recovery Fund Unit Trust

Invests in companies with prospects of recovery which have gone through a difficult period. Aim is capital growth. Accumulation units. Purchased with proceeds from sale of Commercial Union (see entry for Commercial Union). A 20–1 sub-division of units took place in 1990.

Share transfer

When separate taxation of husband and wife was introduced in 1990/1 it was advantageous for many husbands to transfer some of their shares to their wives. This can be achieved without selling and buying the shares, and therefore without incurring any costs, by using the following procedure. Considerable persistance was required to obtain this procedure, which was not available in any of the books, etc. read on investment. It was finally obtained from a helpful company registrar.

Obtain a Stock Transfer Form from a stationer specialising in legal documents or from a bank and fill in the information about the shares, owner and person to whom the shares are being transferred. The last section of the form is titled 'Form of Certificate where Transfer is not Liable to AD VALOREM Stamp Duty' and lists categories (a) to (j). Section (3) asks you to set out the facts explaining the transaction in any case which does not clearly fall within any of the categories (a) to (j). Write here:

> *'Category (L): The conveyance or transfer of property operating as a voluntary disposition inter vivos for no consideration in money.'*

After completion send the form and the share certificate to the Registrar of the company. (Category (L) is printed on forms now.)

Data entry and calculations

The sources for the figures in the performance reviews presented and discussed in this chapter are the three files described in Chapter 9 and the printed Tables 13.2, 13.3 and 13.4. There are differences between the information in the printed tables and on the floppy disk. The data in the printed tables is not as comprehensive as that included in the disk. The latter allows for the recording of information on the numbers and dates on share certificates for instance. This is omitted from the printed tables, since, although it is important to the investor holding the shares, it is of no interest to the reader. The disk contains more frequent data entries than can reasonably be accommodated in the printed tables.

Each table is divided into sections according to the heading on the horizontal axis, and each section is printed on separate sheets of paper. For instance:

Table 13.3: Selected portfolio; share performance.
Table 13.3 (a): Number and scrip.
Table 13.3 (b): Price/share.
Etc.

The performance criteria of the individual shares and the portfolio, presented in this chapter, are calculated over various periods to the end date 30 December 1992. The Tables 13.1 to 13.4 on the floppy disk, however, contain the performance criteria, such as *real growths* and *real returns*, calculated over various periods ending on 31 December 1993. The reasons for choosing different end dates are as follows:

a) By using different end dates on the printed tables and the disk, additional information is made available to the reader.

b) The review period covered in the performance reviews in this chapter is from 31 April 1982 to 30 December 1992. These two dates are at roughly the same stage in the economic recovery from the 1980 and the 1990 recessions. No claim for accuracy is made for the choice of 30 December 1992, but it would certainly be generally accepted that the economic recovery was, relatively, significantly more advanced on 31 December 1993 than it was on 31 April 1982. The choice of a period of time roughly equal to the time between economic cycles gives added meaning to the figures for the performance criteria, and in particular the *target growth* and *target return*.

c) The performance reviews presented in this chapter are intended primarily to inform readers of the way in which such reviews can be constructed, so that they can produce the same type of information for their own portfolios. The actual dates chosen for recording data are of secondary importance.

In view of the small number of shares in each category, the shares in the *selected portfolio* are treated as a single portfolio for assessment purposes. All the information needed to assess the performance of the individual categories (e.g. ordinary, unit trusts and unit trusts (accumulative)) is recorded in Tables 13.2, 13.3 and 13.4, however, so that any investor wishing to carry out such an assessment can do so.

The background knowledge of the market that is needed to fully understand the performance of any portfolio of shares was discussed in Chapter 10. The next two sections of this chapter contain a commentary on the *selected portfolio*, the first concerned with the performance of the individual shares and the second the performance of the portfolio as a whole.

THE PERFORMANCE OF THE INDIVIDUAL SHARES

A performance review of each of the shares in the *selected portfolio* follows this paragraph. The selection of the criteria chosen to be included in such reviews is a matter for personal choice. At its simplest, the review could have comprised only the *real return* figures, as seen in Table 11.12. Alternatively, the reviews could have been extended to include the *real return* in the review tables which follow, and could have covered a wider range of dates.

Commercial Union

From 31 March 1982 until the date of sale on 21 September 1989 the price(c) increasd from 141p to 463p. This apparently good performance is put in perspective by an inspection of the *P/A ratio* in Table 13.3, the ratio having fallen from 1.00 to 0.88 over the same period. On the other hand the *real growth/a* in the share price, between 31 March 1982 and the date of sale, was 11.5 per cent compared with the *target growth/a* of 13.4 per cent. The price on 27 December 1991, 27 months after the sale, was still only 466p, giving a *P/A ratio* of 0.87, whilst on 3 April 1992 it was down to 403p, (*P/A ratio* 0.75). The price and *P/A ratio* on 30 December 1992, however, were 626p and 1.00 respectively, a recovery having taken place. It can be concluded that the timing of the sale was fairly good, although the best option would probably have been to keep the shares until they recovered their value relative to the All Share Index. CGT was payable on the *real gain* of £5,782 less costs and less the tax exemption limit of £5,000 (as it was in 1989/90).

Davis Services

Table 11.1 Davis Services

	Take-over date			
	8/7/87	29/12/89	28/12/90	27/12/91
P/A ratio	1.33	1.19	1.00	1.11
% Real gr/a to 30/12/92	−2.3	2.9	28.2	38.3
% TARG GR/A TO 30/12/92	−2.4	−1.1	10.7	14.7
% Gross yield		5.7	8.9	7.3

Quarterly P/A ratio trend from 5/4/91 to 30/12/92.
1.15, 1.00, 1.12, 1.11, 1.33, 1.38, 1.28, 1.34

On 30/12/92
% Gross yield 5.1 (Target 4.4) P/E ratio 15.7
Real gain £3,440

A takeover resulted in these shares being acquired in place of Sunlight Services in July, 1987, there being an exchange of shares, with no cash payout. Since the takeover the Davis *P/A ratio* fell from 1.33 to 0.88 on 15 February 1991, since when it has risen to 1.34 on 30 December 1992. The *real growth* since the takeover has been negative at −2.3 per cent per annum, but the *target growth* has been almost the same. The performance since the takeover, in terms of *real growth*, can be described as the minimum acceptable, since, although there was a loss in real value the shares did track the All Share Index; the gross yield was high but has fallen recently to 5.1 per cent. The *real gain*, at £3,440, is calculated from the value of the Sunlight Services holding on 31 March 1982, as required by the CGT rules as applied to takeovers.

Marks and Spencer

This is a satisfactory performance, even though the shares under-performed the market in the late 1980s. The recovery, which started

Table 11.2 Marks and Spencer

	31/3/82	31/12/86	29/12/89	28/12/90	27/12/91
P/A ratio	1.12	1.00	0.77	1.00	1.09
% Real gr/a to					
30/12/92	8.7	4.7	12.0	17.4	18.3
% Targ gr/a to					
30/12/92	8.6	2.7	−1.1	10.7	14.7
% Gross yield		3.1	3.7	3.8	3.3

Quarterly P/A ratio trend from 5/4/91 to 30/12/92.
0.97, 0.95, 1.01, 1.09, 1.12, 1.27, 1.24, 1.12.

On 30/12/92
% Gross yield 2.9 (Target 4.4) P/E ratio 20.0
Real gain £2,329

in 1990, continued in 1991, the *real growth/a* at 8.7 per cent over the full period of the review, matching the target. The recent trend in the *P/A ratio* is favourable, although there has been a setback at the turn of the year. The good cover for the dividend (2.3 times) and Marks and Spencer's ability to withstand the recession better than many of its competitors, brought it back into favour with investors. The gross yield is below average at 2.9 per cent, but satisfactory in view of the growth that has taken place. The *real gain* was £2,329 on 30 December 1992, so that no CGT would be incurred on sale.

Sunlight Services

Table 11.3 Sunlight Services

	31/3/82	31/12/86	Takeover 8/7/87
P/A ratio	2.29	1.22	1.33
% Real gr/a from 31/3/82			9.6
% Targ gr/a from 31/3/82			21.5
% Gross yield		6.4	

The performance summary for Davis Services, which took over Sunlight Services on 8 July 1987, should be read in conjunction with these remarks. The rebasing constants have been adjusted so that the *P/A ratio* is the same for both shares on the date of the takeover (see Chapter 5). The *P/A ratio* fell from 2.29 on 31 March 1982 to 1.33 at the time of the takeover, so that Sunlight Services was performing very poorly between 1982 and 1986, compared with the average share in the All Share Index. The early years of this period, particularly, were years of rapid share price increases, whilst inflation was at moderate levels. As a consequence, the *real growth* of the Sunlight Services shares between 31 March 1982 and the date of the takeover was 9.6 per cent per annum compared with the *target growth* of 21.5 per cent per annum.

Whitbread

Table 11.4 Whitbread

	31/3/82	31/12/86	29/12/89	28/12/90	27/12/91
P/A Ratio	0.78	0.74	0.76	1.00	0.83
% Real gr/a to 30/12/92	9.6	5.2	2.8	2.3	17.5
% Targ gr/a to 30/12/92	8.6	2.7	−1.1	10.7	14.7
% Gross yield		4.2	4.3	4.5	5.3

Quarterly P/A ratio trend from 5/4/91 to 30/12/92.
0.90, 0.90, 0.88, 0.83, 0.77, 0.83, 0.86, 0.85.

On 30/12/92
% Gross yield 4.6 (Target 4.4) P/E ratio 13.9
Real gain £2,905

The *P/A ratio* ended the review period at 0.85 compared with 0.78, the figure at which it started, having come near to 1.0 on a number of occasions in the intermediate period. A good performance, with the *real growth* over the full period of the review attaining 9.6 per cent per annum, improving on the *target growth*, although the recent signs of price weakness are rather concerning. The *real gain* was £2,905, but this would only lead to a CGT liability if the Whitbread shares were sold together with another holding.

BAA

Table 11.5 BAA

| | Purchase date | | | |
	21/7/87	29/12/89	28/12/90	27/12/91
P/A ratio	0.74	0.72	1.00	1.13
% Real gr/a to 30/12/92	17.2	25.0	33.4	47.1
% Targ gr/a to 30/12/92	−3.2	−1.1	10.7	14.7
% Gross yield		3.1	3.7	3.3

Quarterly P/A ratio trend from 5/4/91 to 30/12/92.
0.87, 0.95, 0.91, 1.13, 1.21, 1.38, 1.46, 1.45.

On 30/12/92
% Gross yield 2.5 (Target 4.4) P/E ratio 13.9
Real gain £534

Despite the significant but short-lived fall in the share price after launch in 1987, the overall performance has been excellent with a rise in the *P/A ratio* from the purchase figure of 0.74 to 1.45 on 30 December 1992. The *real growth* since purchase has been 17.2 per cent per annum (Target −3.2 per cent per annum). Unfortunately, the number of shares received in the privatisation allocation was small.

ICI

Table 11.6 ICI

	31/3/82	31/12/86	29/12/89	28/12/90	27/12/91
P/A ratio	1.17	1.53	1.12	1.00	1.16
% Real gr/a to 30/12/92	6.3	−5.6	−7.1	6.5	−8.7
% Targ gr/a to 30/12/92	8.6	2.7	−1.1	10.7	14.7
% Gross yield		4.3	5.9	8.4	6.5

Quarterly P/A ratio trend from 5/4/91 to 30/12/92.
1.02, 1.27, 1.23, 1.16, 1.28, 1.19, 1.17, 0.92.

On 30/12/92
% Gross yield 6.9 (target 4.4) P/E ratio 25.5
Real gain £684

Shares in this company were owned by both D and M until 1989 when D's holding was transferred to M (see earlier in this chapter and Table 13.2). The share price analysis is only carried out for one of the holdings. The *P/A ratio* rose from 1.17 on 31 March 1982 to 1.53 on 31 December 1986 and then fell persistently to below 1.0 in the autumn of 1990 before recovering to about 1.28 in early 1992 and then falling to 0.92 at the end of the review period (see Figure 4.1 and Figure 5.1). Over the whole period of the review the *real growth* has been 6.3 per cent per annum, compared with the *target growth* of 8.6 per cent per annum. This is a satisfactory performance. If the shares had been sold on 31 March 1992 however, the 25.6 per cent *real growth/a* achieved from the end of 1990 shows the benefit that could have been achieved by buying before a potential takeover bid becomes apparent to the market and selling before the bid collapses.

Henderson Income & Growth Unit Trust

Table 11.7 Henderson Income & Growth Unit Trust

	31/3/82	31/12/86	29/12/89	28/12/90	27/12/91
P/A ratio	0.89	1.03	1.04	1.00	0.92
% Real gr/a to 30/12/92	9.0	0.8	−4.9	6.3	15.1
% Targ gr/a to 30/12/92	8.6	2.7	−1.1	10.7	14.7
% Gross yield		3.4	4.0	6.3	5.7

Quarterly P/A ratio trend from 5/4/91 to 30/12/92.
1.02, 0.98, 0.98, 0.92, 0.93, 0.94, 0.92, 0.92.

On 30/12/92
% Gross yield 4.3 (target 4.4) Real gain £9,579

The *P/A ratio* rose from 0.89 on 31 March 1982 to 0.92 on 30 December 1992, having reached 1.08 at the end of 1988. The recent fall in the *P/A ratio* is attributed to a disproportionate holding of small-company shares. The *real growth* was 9.0 per cent per annum over the full review period, compared with a *target growth* of 8.6 per cent per annum, the major part of the growth taking place in the first couple of years. The gross yield has fallen to 4.3 per cent from about 6 per cent in the first two years of this decade. The Henderson Income and Growth UT performance over the years can be classified as good. The *real gain* outstripped the CGT exemption in the early 1980s, and now stands at £9,579, but there seems to be no reason to consider disposing of this investment, other than a dire need for cash!

Invesco Great British Companies Unit Trust

Table 11.8 Invesco Great British Companies Unit Trust

	31/3/82	31/12/86	29/12/89	28/12/90	27/12/91
P/A ratio	1.04	1.05	1.06	1.00	1.05
% Real gr/a to					
30/12/92	8.5	2.3	−2.1	12.3	12.0
% Targ gr/a to					
30/12/92	8.6	2.7	−1.1	10.7	14.7
% Gross yield		2.5	4.0	3.3	3.1

Quarterly P/A ratio trend from 5/4/91 to 30/12/92.
1.00, 1.03, 1.02, 1.05, 1.07, 1.07, 1.04, 1.03.

On 30/12/92
% Gross yield 1.8 (target 4.4) Real gain £1,168

Save & Prosper Investment Trust Unit Trust

Table 11.9 Save & Prosper Investment Trust Unit Trust

	31/3/82	31/12/86	29/12/89	28/12/90	27/12/91
P/A ratio	1.00	1.05	1.07	1.00	1.01
% Real gr/a to					
30/12/92	8.8	2.2	−2.6	11.8	16.3
% Targ gr/a to					
30/12/92	8.6	2.7	−1.1	10.7	14.7
% Gross yield		2.6	2.2	3.2	2.1

Quarterly P/A ratio trend from 5/4/91 to 30/12/92.
1.01, 1.05, 1.03, 1.01, 1.03, 0.96, 0.98, 1.02.

On 30/12/92
% Gross yield 1.8 (target 4.4) Real gain £4,532

The *P/A ratio* more than maintained its level over the full review period, having varied little over the years. The *real growth* over the same period was 8.5 per cent per annum, matching the target, although over the last year it has fallen short of the target. The gross yield, however, was less than target throughout the review period, falling to only 1.8 per cent on 30 December 1992, so that the overall performance can be classified as satisfactory/good.

The *P/A ratio* has increased slightly over the 10 years to 30 December 1992, whilst the *real growth* has slightly improved on the target. The gross yield was only 1.8 per cent on 30 December 1992, the low value presumably being the price paid for the extra security of the wide spread of investments achieved with this Save and Prosper UT, which is invested in investment trusts; an overall performance that can be classified as between satisfactory and good.

M & G Compound Growth Unit Trust (Acc)

Table 11.10 M & G Compound Growth Unit Trust (Acc)

	31/3/82	31/12/86	29/12/89	28/12/90	27/12/91
P/A ratio	1.01	0.95	1.02	1.00	0.97
% Real ret/a to 30/12/92	9	4	−2	11	19
% Targ ret/a to 30/12/92	12	6	3	14	18
% Gross yield (re-inv'd)		3.3	3.9	6.9	4.8

Quarterly P/A ratio trend from 5/4/91 to 30/12/92.
0.99, 1.00, 0.99, 0.97, 1.01, 1.04, 1.00, 1.01.

On 30/12/92
% Gross yield 3.6(reinvested) (target 4.4)

The *P/A ratio* has exactly retained its level of 1.01 from beginning to end of the review period, a poor performance in view of the fact that the dividends were reinvested. Accumulation unit trusts are best analysed by monitoring the *real* and *target returns* rather than the *real* and *target growths*, (Chapter 5). Over the full review period this unit trust achieved a *real return* of only 9 per cent per annum compared with the *target return* of 12 per cent per annum.

M & G Recovery Unit Trust (Acc)

Table 11.11 M & G Recovery Unit Trust (Acc)

	Purchase date 21/9/89	29/12/89	28/12/90	27/12/91
P/A ratio	1.17	1.06	1.00	0.94
% Real ret/a to 30/12/92	−6	−3	11	23
% Targ ret/a to 30/12/92	2	3	14	18
% Gross yield		4.3	5.7	5.4

Quarterly P/A ratio trend from 5/4/91 to 30/12/92.
1.01, 0.99, 1.01, 0.94, 0.98, 1.01, 0.96, 1.00.

On 30/12/92
% Gross yield 3.9(reinvested) (target 4.4)

These units were received from M & G in exchange for the Commercial Union shares in 1989, thereby saving buying and selling charges. The *P/A ratio* has fallen from 1.17 on the date of purchase to 1.00 on 30 December 1992, despite the reinvestment of the dividends. The *real return* over the two and a half years since purchase has been −6 per cent per annum, a very large loss, although it does, of course, include the costs of buying. The performance has also been poor when compared with the All Share Index, since the *target return* over the same period was 2 per cent per annum. Roughly one-third of the difference is accounted for by the buying costs and the remaining two-thirds by the heavy loading of small and potential recovery companies in this unit trust. As already mentioned, the timing of the disposal of the insurance company shares was reasonable, but the purchase of the Recovery units was premature, the downturn in the prices of the companies in the M&G Recovery Unit Trust portfolio since purchase being greater than expected. The hope is that the performance of unit trusts of this type will be better than the average when the economy does begin to expand.

Comparative performance

Some investors might prefer an even more concise, comparative summary of the performance of the individual shares, of the type shown in Table 11.12. The reasons for the difference between the figures for the average of the *real return* of the individual shares and the *real return* of the portfolio as a whole, are discussed in more detail in the next section and in Appendix 6.

Table 11.12 gives the *real returns* of the shares and the portfolio over a range of years, all ending on 30 December 1992. This is the same end date as has been used for the performance reviews of the individual shares reported earlier in this chapter.

There is seen to be quite large differences between the performances of the various shares, particularly the ordinary shares. The unit

Table 11.12. Real return of shares in selected portfolio

Years to 30/12/92	8	6	3	I
		% Real return per annum		
DavisServ			8	42
MarksSp	10	7	14	20
Whitbread	8	9	6	21
BAA			27	49
ICI	4	−1	−2	−3
HendInGr	8	4	−1	18
InvGrBrC	7	4	0	13
SPInvTr	7	4	−1	18
MGCompGr	6	4	−2	19
MGRec'y			−3	23
Average	7	5	5	22
Target	9	6	3	18
Portfolio	8	6	I	23

trusts, other than over the last year, have fallen short of target performance. This is despite the fact that these particular unit trusts in the *selected portfolio* are all above average performers over the longer term, compared with unit trusts in general, (see Appendix 5). The portfolio as a whole has almost matched the performance of the All Share Index, the shortfall over the last three years being followed by the good performance over the last year.

THE PERFORMANCE OF THE PORTFOLIO

The performance figures of the *selected portfolio* as a whole are summarised in Table 11.12 and below in Table 11.13 and shown in Figure 11.1.

There are not enough shares in each category to make it worthwhile to calculate the performance by category. The comments therefore apply to the whole of the *selected portfolio*. Over the full

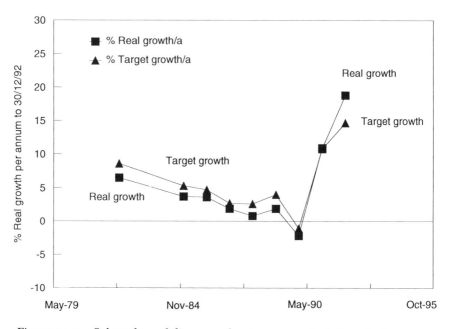

Figure 11.1   Selected portfolio: growth rates over periods to 30/12/92

Table 11.13 Summary of the selected portfolio performance

	% Real growth p.a.		% Yield (net)		% Real return p.a.	
	Portf'o	Target	Portf'o	Target	Portf'o	Target
Periods to 30/12/92						
31/3/82	6.5	8.6				
29/12/84	3.7	5.3	3.4	3.1	8	9
31/12/85	3.6	4.7	3.3	3.0	8	8
31/12/86	1.9	2.7	3.2	2.9	6	6
29/12/87	0.8	2.6	3.1	3.1	5	6
30/12/88	1.9	4.0	3.5	3.2	6	8
29/12/89	−2.2	−1.1	3.5	3.2	1	3
28/12/90	10.9	10.7	4.5	4.1	15	14
27/12/91	18.8	14.7	4.2	3.9	23	18
30/12/92			3.5	3.3		

Definitions:

The *real growth* was determined by the direct (T&E) method.

The *real return* was determined by the direct (IRR) method.

period of the review the *real growth* was 6.5 per cent per annum compared with a *target growth* of 8.6 per cent, whilst the yield was only slightly higher than the *target yield*. The *real return* of the whole portfolio over the shorter periods was also less than or equal to target, except over the last two years. A quick inspection of the *real return* and *target return* figures for each share in Table 11.12 and the summary in the last chapter, leads to the following reasons for the performance of the portfolio being poorer than target:

a) The performance of the Commercial Union and Sunlight Services shares, particularly the latter, were poor compared to the All Share Index, as demonstrated by the following figures:

	% Growth p.a. from 31/3/82 to date of sale	
	Real	*Target*
ComUnion	11.5	13.4
SunServ	9.6	21.5

b) The M & G Recovery shares have not performed well since purchase, partly because of the 5 per cent difference between the bid and offer prices. The *real return* since purchase was −6 per cent per annum compared with the target of 2 per cent per annum. Buying costs will always have this effect, of course, in the short term. It should be noted that the buying costs will affect the *real growth* of the portfolio but not the target growth or the average of the *real returns* shown in Table 11.13.

c)   The performance of the M & G Compound Growth shares was disappointing, at least partly as a result of the emphasis on smaller companies.

d)   The performance of the ICI shares was poor throughout most of the review period. This would have the effect of bringing down the average more than the portfolio performance, since the holding of ICI shares was relatively small.

e)   The very good performance of the BAA shares had a greater effect on the average than on the whole portfolio performance, because of the small size of the BAA holding.

In summary, the performance of the portfolio over the eight years, with a *real return* of 8 per cent per annum, can be classed as satisfactory, since the *target return* was 9 per cent. The *real return* on the three-month inter-bank rate over the same eight years was only 3 per cent per annum.

There is reason to believe that the performance of the *selected portfolio* will improve in future as the economy emerges from the recession and the smaller companies start performing in the way they did in the 1980s. The figures in Table 11.13 indicate that this improvement has already started, the *real return* over 1992 having been five points higher than the *target return* (see next section).

PERFORMANCE DATA FROM THE FLOPPY DISK

The printed Tables 13.2, 13.3 and 13.4, and the review so far carried out, of the information that can be gathered from these tables, has concerned the performance of the shares and the *selected portfolio* up to the end of December, 1992. Tables 13.2, 13.3 and 13.4 are recorded on the floppy disk, but in this case the review period ends on

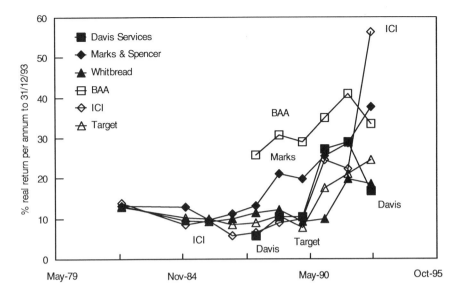

Figure 11.2   Ordinary shares: % real returns/a – periods to 31/12/93

31 December, 1993. The real returns of the shares in the *selected portfolio* are shown graphically in Figures 11.2 and 11.3.

Table 11.14 summarises some of the results for those shares which have been held since 31 March, 1982. The *real returns* of the shares range from 10 to 14 per cent per annum over the almost 12 years of the review, giving an average of 13 per cent per annum, which matches the *target return*. The *real returns* over the full period of the review are more consistent than expected. The results over the last year were more variable, but the average comfortably exceeded the target.

Of the shares held for shorter periods, the BAA shares have been outstanding, showing a *real growth* of 15.7 per cent per annum (target 0.2) over the six years since purchase. The M&G Recovery units, after a poor start, have grown at an appreciably higher rate than the target over the last two years, but the *real growth* since purchase is still below target. The Davis Services shares have matched the target since the date they were received as a result of a takeover.

The *real return* on a savings account, earning interest at the three-month inter-bank rate, would only have been 3 per cent per annum

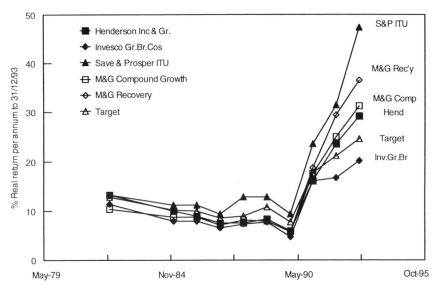

Figure 11.3   Unit trusts: % real return/a – periods to 31/12/93

Table 11.14 The real return of shares to 31 December 1993

	%Real return / annum to 31/12/93	
From	31/03/82	30/12/92
MarksSp	13	38
Whitbread	13	19
ICI	14	56
HendInGr	13	29
InvGrBrC	11	20
SPInvTr	13	47
MGCompGr	10	31
Average	13	34
Target	13	25

over the full period of the review, compared with the *target return* for shares of 13 per cent per annum (see Table 13.1 on the disk). These results confirm that shares are a much better investment than bank or building society savings accounts, providing there is no risk of them having to be sold unexpectedly, at short notice.

12

THE PERFORMANCE OF FIXED INTEREST INVESTMENTS

'He thought he saw a Banker's Clerk
Descending from the 'bus:
He looked again, and found it was
A Hippopotamus.
"If this should stay to dine," he said,
"There won't be much for us!" '
Lewis Carroll, 1832–1898

There is a very wide variety of fixed-interest (FI) investments, ranging from the bank deposit account to the gilt-edged security.

They can be classified according to whether they can be purchased at face value, cashed at face value at any time or at a fixed date in the future, receive interest at a fixed rate or at a rate that can be altered at any time, etc. The *real return* per annum is more suited to performance assessment for FI investments than the *real growth* per annum and the yield, for the following reasons:

a) Investments which are purchased and sold at their face value will have a negative *real growth*, due to inflation. This adds to the complexity of interpretation of performance for the private investor.

b) The range of *real growths* and yields will be much greater than for equities.

The recommended method chosen for inclusion in the System is, therefore, to calculate the *real return*.

FI investments can be divided into two groups; firstly those such as bank and building society savings accounts, which retain their face value and therefore normally show a negative real rate of growth. They are only attractive as investments because the yield is usually much higher than for equities and they can be converted into a predetermined amount of cash at short notice. The performance of a bank or building society savings account is compared with the performance of the average share, as represented by the All Share Index, in Chapter 10, Table 13.1 and Figures 10.1 and 10.2. The *real return* on a savings account, earning interest at the three-month inter-bank rate, was 3 per cent per annum for much of the 1980s, rising to 5 per cent in the early 1990s, but has recently been falling.

The second group comprises those investments which are traded on the stock exchange. Both the purchase price and the sale price vary according to demand. Many investments in this second group, including the majority of preference shares, loan stock and gilt-edged securities, have a nominated date on which the investment is repaid at face value. The performance of investments of this type can best be measured by using the same methods as those developed for equities. The performance to redemption can also be calculated by entering forecast rates of inflation between the current date and the redemption date.

Table 12.1 shows an example of the calculation of the *real return* of a fixed interest investment of the second type, where the value of the stock varies according to supply and demand.

The growth in the real value of the investment, with net interest reinvested, i.e the *real return* has been 4, 6 and 6 per cent per annum, over three, two and one year(s) respectively.

A suitable standard of comparison for both types of fixed interest investment is the index-linked gilt, which in the past has yielded 3 to 4 per cent to redemption, and maintains the real value of the initial investment. Other factors, such as the security of the company or organisation that has issued the stock must, of course, also be taken into account. A private company, however high its credit rating, cannot be as secure as a government stock; further-

Table 12.1   The performance of fixed interest investments

Year end	8% Loan Stock (£1) 1987	Net interest 1988	1989	6.0 % 1990
Share price,p.	50	47	47	48
Net yield,%	12.0	12.8	12.8	12.5
Period to End 1990				
% Price growth/a	−1.4	1.1	2.1	
% Real growth/a	**−8.7**	**−6.8**	**−6.5**	
% Real return/a	**4**	**6**	**6**	
RPI	103.3	110.6	119.1	130.1
% Infl to end 1990	8.0	8.5	9.2	

Definitions:

a) Net yield = Net interest / Price per share
b) Price growth/a = @ Rate (Price(end 1990), Price(x), Years) where x is the date
    at the top of the column.
c) Real growth/a = (Price gr/a − Infl) / (1 + Infl/100)
d) Real return/a = Real growth/a + avg. net yield

more, the index-linked gilt is protected against rapidly escalating
inflation. A higher *real return* than 4 per cent per annum must
therefore be expected from preference shares, loan stocks, etc.
Another suitable standard is the *real return* on a savings account
earning interest at the three-month interbank rate, (see Table 13.1).
The *real return* on such an account was 3 per cent per annum over
most of the 1980s, rising to 5 per cent per annum in the early 1990s. It
has recently been falling. The performance of the loan stock shown
in Table 12.1 is moving towards the satisfactory range, therefore, but
still has some distance to go.

In general the *real return* on investments increases as the risk
increases. They can be ranked in order of increasing risk and *real
return* as follows:

Index-linked gilt-edged stock.
Gilt-edged stock.
Bank and building society accounts.
Preference shares, loan stocks, etc.
Unit trusts and investment trusts.
Equity shares.
Options/warrants.

13

SUMMARY OF THE SYSTEM

Lord Kelvin (1824–1907) believed that little could be known about any subject unless it could be measured.

The following criteria, for assessing share and portfolio performance, have been chosen for inclusion in the System. The targets corresponding to each of the criteria are also listed.

The tables in which the chosen criteria for the *selected portfolio* can be found, are noted. The performance figures for the individual shares are in the *MspPri* file, whilst those for the portfolio are in the *MspPort* file.

The criteria chosen for individual shares are as follows:

- *P/A ratio*, Table 13.3(d).
- *Real gain*,£, Table 13.3(e): criterion for comparison: CGT exemption limit.
- Price / earnings ratio, Table13.3(f).
- %Gross yield, Table 13.3(g): criterion for comparison: *%target yield*.
- *Real growth*, over various periods to end date. Tables 13.3(j) or 13.3(l): criterion for comparison: *target growth*.
- *Real return*, over various periods to end date, Table 13.3(k): criterion for comparison: *target return*.

The criteria chosen for portfolios are as follows:

- %Net yield, Table 13.4(e): criterion for comparison: *%target yield (net)*.
- *Real growth*, over past year and various periods to end date, Tables 13.4(g): criterion for comparison: *target growth*.

- *Real return*, over various periods to end date, Table 13.4(h): criterion for comparison: *target return*.

The criteria chosen for Peps, where the dividends are reinvested, are as follows:

- *Real return*, over various periods to end date, Tables 13.4(g) or 13.4(h): criterion for comparison: *target return*.

The criteria adopted for monitoring the performance of fixed interest investments are as follows:

- *Real return*, over various periods to end date.
- *Real return* to redemption date: criteria for comparison: *Real return* on index-linked gilts; *Real return* on three-month bank rate; *Target return*.

The end date is the last date of the review period. Readers are reminded that they have a choice, between two different methods of calculation, in determining the *real growth* and the *real return* of portfolios i.e. the T&E or the IRR methods.

Different investors will have different views on the criteria chosen for inclusion in the System, depending upon the time they have available, their computer and software, their portfolio, etc. This book has aimed to give investors a wide range of methods of performance assessment from which to choose, only some of which are listed in this section. Many methods, which at first sight have attractive features, were tried and found wanting in some respect and are not therefore to be found in the book. Those included in the System were only chosen after much careful thought and trial use.

Table 13.1 Market statistics (File: MspMktSt)

	31/03/82	29/12/84	31/12/85	31/12/86	29/12/87	30/12/88
Equities						
30 Share	560	945	1133	1309	1383	1455
100 Share	725	1225	1414	1673	1730	1793
AlShI	323	590	682	833	891	926
RPI	80.2	91.0	96.1	99.8	103.3	110.6
Tax % (Basic)	30	30	30	29	27	25
Targ yield,%						
Gross	5.8	4.4	4.3	4.1	4.2	4.6
Net	4.1	3.1	3.0	2.9	3.1	3.5
AlShI/30Sh	1.00	1.08	1.04	1.10	1.12	1.10
AlShI/100Sh	1.00	1.08	1.08	1.12	1.16	1.16
AlShI/RPI	1.00	1.61	1.76	2.07	2.14	2.08
Past Year						
% Infl./a		4.7	5.6	3.9	3.5	7.1
% AlShI gr/a		24.3	15.6	22.1	7.0	3.9
%Targ gr/a		18.7	9.5	17.6	3.3	−2.9
%Targ ret/a		22	12	21	6	1
Period to	30/12/92					
Years	10.8	8.0	7.0	6.0	5.0	4.0
% Infl/a	5.2	5.4	5.4	5.6	6.0	5.8
% AlShI gr/a	14.3	11.0	10.3	8.5	8.8	10.0
%Targ gr./a	8.6	5.3	4.7	2.7	2.6	4.0
%Targ ret/a	12	9	8	6	6	8
£ sterling						
%IntBank rate	13.7	9.9	11.9	11.2	8.9	13.0
%IntBank(net)	9.6	6.9	8.3	8.0	6.5	9.8
Past year						
%Real gr/a		−4.5	−5.3	−3.7	−3.4	−6.6
%Real ret/a		2	3	4	3	3
Period to	30/12/92					
%Real gr/a	−5.0	−5.1	−5.1	−5.3	−5.7	−5.5
%Real ret/a	3	3	3	3	3	4

Definitions:

Equities, performance over past year:

% Inflation/a. (Infl) = (RPI(y) − RPI(x)) × 100 / RPI(x)

% All Share Index growth/a. (AlShIGr) = (AlShI(y) − AlShI(x)) × 100 / AlShI(x)

x and y are dates at the tops of the columns, one year apart.

Table 13.1 Market statistics, continued

	07/04/89	29/12/89	06/04/90	29/06/90	28/09/90	28/12/90
Equities						
30 Share	1683	1917	1740	1900	1536	1685
100 Share	2046	2423	2221	2375	1990	2160
AlShI	1059	1205	1103	1171	962	1038
RPI	113.8	119.1	124.0	126.8	129.7	130.1
Basic tax,%	25	25	25	25	25	25
Targ yield,%						
Gross		4.2	4.9	4.7	5.8	5.4
Net		3.2	3.7	3.5	4.4	4.1
AlShI/30Sh	1.09	1.09	1.10	1.07	1.09	1.07
AlShI/100Sh	1.16	1.12	1.12	1.11	1.09	1.08
AlShI/RPI	2.31	2.51	2.21	2.30	1.84	1.98
Past year						
% Infl/a		7.7	9.0			9.2
% AlShI gr/a		30.1	4.2			−13.8
% Targ gr/a		20.8	−4.4			−21.1
% Targ ret/a		24	−1			−17
Period to 30/12/92						
Years	3.7	3.0	2.7	2.5	2.3	2.0
% Infl/a	5.4	5.2	4.2	3.6	3.0	3.2
% AlShI gr/a	6.9	4.1	7.9	6.1	16.5	14.3
% Targ gr/a	1.4	−1.1	3.6	2.4	13.1	10.7
% Targ ret/a		3	7	6	17	14
£ sterling						
% Int bank rate		15.1	15.1	14.9	14.9	14.0
% Int Bank(net)		11.3	11.3	11.2	11.2	10.5
Past Year						
% Real gr/a		−7.1	−8.2			−8.5
% Real ret/a		4	3			2
Period to 30/12/92						
% Real gr./a	−5.1	−4.9	−4.0	−3.5	−2.9	−3.1
% Real ret/a		3	4	4	4	4

Definitions: (cont.)

Equities, performance over years to 30/12/92

Infl = @Rate (RPI(30/12/92), RPI(x), Years)

% Growth in All Share Index (AlShI gr) = @Rate (AlShI(30/12/92), AlShI(x), Years) × 100

% Target growth = (AlShIGrowth − Infl) / (1 + Infl/100)

% Target return = % Target growth + average % target yield (net)

Table 13.1 Market statistics, continued

	05/04/91	28/06/91	27/09/91	27/12/91	03/04/92	26/06/92
Equities						
30 Share	2015	1878	2019	1842	1851	1964
100 Share	2545	2415	2599	2419	2383	2534
AlShI	1232	1161	1258	1157	1142	1224
RPI	132.7	134.0	134.7	135.7	137.8	139.1
Basic tax,%	25	25	25	25	25	25
Targ yield,%						
Gross	4.6	5.1	4.7	5.2	5.2	4.9
Net	3.5	3.8	3.5	3.9	3.9	3.6
AlShI/30Sh	1.06	1.07	1.08	1.09	1.07	1.08
AlShI/100Sh	1.09	1.08	1.09	1.07	1.08	1.09
AlShI/RPI	2.31	2.15	2.32	2.12	2.06	2.19
Past Year						
% Infl/a	7.0	5.7	3.9	4.3	3.8	3.8
%AlShI gr/a	11.7	−0.9	30.7	11.4	−7.3	5.4
%Targ gr/a	4.4	−6.2	25.8	6.8	−10.7	1.5
%Targ ret/a	8	−2	29	11	−7	5
Period to 30/12/92						
Years	1.7	1.5	1.3	1.0	0.7	0.5
% Infl/a	2.5	2.3	2.3	2.1	0.8	−0.7
%AlShI gr/a	5.7	10.9	6.3	17.2	26.2	22.5
%Targ gr./a	3.1	8.5	3.9	14.7	25.2	23.3
%Targ ret/a	7	12	7	18		
£ sterling						
%Intbank Rate	12.2	11.3	10.2	10.9	11.1	10.2
%Intbank(net)	9.2	8.5	7.7	8.2	8.3	7.6
Past Year						
%Real gr/a	−6.6	−5.4	−3.7	−4.1	−3.7	−3.7
%Real ret/a	3	3	4	4	5	4
Period to 30/12/92						
%Real gr/a	−2.5	−2.2	−2.2	−2.1	−0.8	0.7
%Real ret/a	5	4	4	3		

Definitions: (cont.)

Bank Account:
The interest rate recorded for the bank account is the three-month inter-bank rate.

% Real growth = (% Price growth − Infl) / (1 + Infl/100)

When measuring the % real growth of a bank deposit, the % price growth is zero, since it is assumed that the interest is withdrawn. The % real growth is, of course negative as a result of the effect of inflation. When measuring the real growth over the past year, the % inflation over the past year is used in the above equation. For the real growth over the years to 30/12/92, the % Inflation to 30/12/92 is used.

%Real return = %Real growth + % Net yield (avg.)

For the bank account, the net yield is equal to the net Inter-bank interest rate.

Table 13.1 Market statistics, continued

	25/09/92	30/12/92	02/04/93	02/07/93	01/10/93	31/12/93
Equities						
30 Share	1914	2171	2223	2238	2313	2560
100 Share	2601	2833	2870	2858	3039	3418
AlShI	1228	1358	1405	1417	1507	1682
RPI	139.6	138.6	140.0	140.8	140.8	142.0
Basic tax,%	25	25	25	20	20	20
Targ yield,%						
Gross	4.8	4.4	4.2	3.9	3.8	3.4
Net	3.6	3.3	3.1	3.1	3.0	2.7
AlShI/30Sh	1.11	1.09	1.10	1.10	1.13	1.14
AlShI/100Sh	1.06	1.08	1.10	1.11	1.11	1.11
AlShI/RPI	2.19	2.44	2.49	2.50	2.66	2.94
Past Year						
% Infl/a	3.6	2.1	1.6	1.2	0.9	2.5
%AlShI Gr/a	−2.3	17.4	23.0	15.8	22.7	23.9
%Targ gr/a	−5.8	14.9	21.1	14.4	21.6	20.9
%Targ ret/a	−2	18	24	17	25	24
Period to 30/12/92						
Years	0.3					
% Infl/a	−2.7					
%AlShI gr/a	46.6					
%Targ gr/a	50.7					
%Targ ret/a						
£ sterling						
%Int bank rate	9.3	7.1	5.9	5.8	5.9	5.3
%Int bank(net)	6.9	5.3	4.4	4.7	4.8	4.2
Past year						
%Real gr./a	−3.5	−2.1	−1.6	−1.2	−1.6	−2.4
%Real ret/a	3	3	3	3	3	2
Period to	30/12/92					
%Real gr./a	2.8					
%Real ret/a						

Table 13.2(a) Selected portfolio: data (File: MspData)

Company	Owner	Cat'y	Nom'l value p.	Year- end	Date Divi Paid inter	final	How obtain
CommUn'n	D	Ord	25	31/12			Purch
DavisServ	D	Ord	25	31/12	27/10	13/6	T/O
ICI	D	Ord	100	7/8			Purch
MarksSp	D	Ord	25	31/3	26/1	18/8	Purch
SunServ	D	Ord	10				Purch
Whitbread	D	Ord	25	25/2	5/1	28/7	Purch
BAA	M	Ord	25	31/3	22/1	8/8	Purch
ICI	M	Ord	100	31/12	28/4	2/10	Pur/Tr
HendInGr	D	UT		21/5	21/1	21/7	Purch
InvGrBrC	M	UT		1/1	1/3	1/9	Purch
SPInvTr	M	UT		30/9	31/5	30/11	Purch
MGCompGr	D	UTAcc		27/4		27/4	Purch
MGRec'y	M	UTAcc		30/6		20/8	Purch

Table 13.2(a) Selected portfolio: data continued

Company	As at 31/3/82 Number	Price p.	Value £.	Purchased No. Tot	Price p.	Date	Cost £.
CommUn'n	2280	141	3215				
DavisServ				5597	174	8/7/87	9722
ICI	112	318	356				
MarksSp	600	155	930				
SunServ	2946	160	4714				
Whitbread	940	107	1006				
BAA				100	245	21/7/87	100
ICI	135	318	429	112	1050	13/2/89	1176
HendInGr	7350	49	3631				
InvGrBrC	440	110	485				
SPInvTr	5025	35	1774				
MGCompGr	1686	174	2940				
MGRec'y				1090	992	21/9/89	10812
Total			19480				21810

Abbreviations:
Purchase (Purch)
Takeover (T/O)
Purchase and Transfer (Pur/Tr)

Notes:
    Categories classified as shares are:
    Ordinary shares
    Unit Trusts
    Unit Trust (Accumulative)
    Investment Trusts
There are no Investment Trusts in the Selected Portfolio. If there were, they would
be treated in exactly the same way as ordinary shares, except that the net asset value
and the discount or premium should be recorded in the 'MspPri' file.

Prices on 31/3/82 from FT publication CGT, (calculated as at March 1988), but
re-calculated to show actual prices at 31/3/82 (see Chapter 5 on corrected prices).

Mid-market prices are used for ord. shares, bid prices for Unit Trusts.

The price shown in the 'Purchased-TotPrice' column is the price paid per share on
purchase. When payments are phased, this is the total price.

The figures shown in the 'Purchased-Cost,£' column are the costs of purchase,
including stamp duty, charges, etc. When payments are phased, this column contains
the first phase payment.

When a company is taken over and the shares exchanged, no money changing hands,
the selling price of the shares in the company that has been taken-over is taken as
equal to the cash offer. This allows a value to be put on the shares, which, in turn,
allows a value to be put on the shares in the takeover company.

Table 13.2(a) Selected portfolio: data continued

Company	Purchased					
	AlShI	RPI	Date	Cost £.	AlShI	RPI
CommUn'n						
DavisServ	1143	101.8				
ICI						
MarksSp						
SunServ						
Whitbread						
BAA	1200	101.8	4/5/88	145	920	106.0
ICI	1070	112.0				
HendInGr						
InvGrBrC						
SPInvTr						
MGCompGr						
MGRec'y	1202	117.0				
Total				145		

Table 13.2(a) Selected portfolio: data continued

Company	Extra Purchased			
	Number	Price p	Date	Cost £.
CommUn'n	55	300	15/5/87	165
DavisServ				
ICI				
MarksSp	10	234	17/1/91	23
SunServ				
Whitbread				
BAA				
ICI				
HendInGr				
InvGrBrC				
SPInvTr				
MGCompGr				
MGRec'y				
Total				188

Notes continued:

The ICI shares held by 'D' were transferred to 'M' on 13/2/89.

The second group of columns under the 'Purchased' heading are used for second phase payments. An example is the purchase of BAA shares for which there were two phased payments.

The 'Extra Purchased' heading covers the situation where a second tranche of share are purchased, the first tranche being recorded as already held on 31/3/82 or being recorded under the 'Purchased' heading. The columns under the heading 'Extra Purchased' can be repeated as often as necessary.

Shares purchased by reinvesting the dividends or from rights issues, are recorded in these columns as well as straightforward purchases.

The 'Received,£' figure is the net amount received from the sale of the shares.

Godfrey Davis (now Davis Services) took over Sunlight Services on 8/7/87. There was a straightforward share exchange, no cash being paid.

The proceeds from the sale of the Commercial union shares were immediately invested in the M & G Recovery unit trust accumulation units. M & G implemented the sale and purchase without charge. The dates of income distribution are those which would have applied if the units had not been accumulation units.

The ICI shares transferred to M from D were treated as sold by D and purchased by M, at the market price on the date of transfer.

Under the 'Scrip Issues' heading, the Ratio is the number of new shares issued for the number held already. The 'Number' is the number of new shares issued.

At the end of June, 1993, ICI demerged into ICI and Zeneco.

Under the heading 'Total no.' is recorded the total number of shares held, however they were acquired.

The 'Nom val' heading allows for the recording of the current nominal value of the shares.

Table 13.2(a) Selected portfolio: data continued

Company	Sold Number	Price p.	Date	Received £.	AlShI	RPI
CommUn'n	2335	463	21/9/89	10811	1202	117.0
DavisServ						
ICI	112	1050	13/2/89	1176	1070	112.0
MarksSp						
SunServ	2946	330	8/7/87	9722	1143	101.8
Whitbread						
BAA						
ICI						
HendInGr						
InvGrBrC						
SPInvTr						
MGCompGr						
MGRec'y						
Total				21709		

Table 13.2(a) Selected portfolio: data continued

Company	Scrip issues			Current holding	
	Ratio	Number	Date	Total no	Nom val
CommUn'n					
DavisServ				5597	25
ICI					
MarksSp	1for1	600	27/7/84	1210	25
SunServ					
Whitbread				940	25
BAA	1for10	10	31/7/90	110	25
ICI	1 Zeneca for 1 ICI		1/6/93	247	100
HendInGr				7350	
InvGrBrC	9for1	3960	2/7/89	4400	
SPInvTr				5025	
MGCompGr				1686	
MGRec'y	19for1	20710	25/6/90	21800	

Table 13.2(b)

Company	Invested, £ 31/03/82	29/12/84	31/12/85	31/12/86	29/12/87	30/12/88	29/12/89	28/12/90	27/12/91	30/12/92	31/12/93
CommUn'n	3215				165		−10811				
DavisServ					9722						
ICI	356						−1176				
MarksSp	930								23		
SunServ	4714				−9722						
Whitbread	1006										
BAA					100	145					
ICI	429						1176				
HendInGr	3631										
InvGrBrC	485										
SPInvTr	1774										
MGCompGr	2940	199	128	152	179	184	208	357	344	337	349
MGRec'y							10811	331	353	288	274
Total	19480	199	128	152	444	329	208	687	721	625	624

Notes:

Sales are recorded as negative investments.

The figures recorded in the 'Invested' columns opposite each company are the investments in the period ending on the date at the top of the column and beginning on the date at the top of the previous column.

In the case of UT (Acc) shares, such as M & G Compound Growth and M & G Recovery, the net dividends are recorded in the appropriate 'Invested' column.

Table 13.2(c)

Company	Invested fraction										
	31/03/82	29/12/84	31/12/85	31/12/86	29/12/87	30/12/88	29/12/89	28/12/90	27/12/91	30/12/92	31/12/93
CommUn'n					108		−2992				
DavisServ					4688						
ICI							−1034				
MarksSp									22		
SunServ					−4688						
Whitbread											
BAA					45	96					
ICI							1034				
HendInGr											
InvGrBrC											
SPInvTr											
MGCompGr		135	87	103	122	125	142	242	234	229	237
MGRec'y							2992	207	222	181	172
Total		135	87	103	274	221	142	450	478	410	409

Notes:
The Invested fraction is defined as:
InvFract = Inv × Days to end of year / 365 where Inv = net invested in year and Days = number of days between date of purchase and year end.

Computer Tips: Tables 13.3(a) to 13.3(g)

The form in which the information in Table 13.3 is recorded requires a generous allocation of space. This is particularly true of Table 13.3(a), where the numbers of four of the companies are unchanged from the start date to the end date.

This form is chosen because it makes the formulation of the equations and the calculations easy. This is also the reason for calculating and recording the net yield. It would have been possible to calculate the return directly from the gross yield (and the growth rate), but this would have been more complicated.

Dates are all entered using the Lotus @Date function. This means that the date is represented by a serial number, so that the number of days or years between dates is easily calculated.

Note the difference between 'Copy' and 'Copy Values' in these computer tips. 'Copy' will copy formulas. 'Copy Values' will copy to the new address only the mathematical value of the cell being copied, and not the formula.

Table 13.3(a) Selected portfolio: share performance. File: MspPri

Company	31/03/82 Number & Scrip	29/12/84	31/12/85	31/12/86	29/12/87	30/12/88	29/12/89	28/12/90	27/12/91	26/06/92	25/09/92	30/12/92
CommUn'n	2280	2280	2280	2280	2280	2280						
DavisServ					5597	5597	5597	5597	5597	5597	5597	5597
ICI	112	112	112	112	112	112						
MarksSp	600	1200	1200	1200	1200	1200	1200	1200	1200	1200	1200	1200
SunServ	2946	2946	2946	2946								
Whitbread	940	940	940	940	940	940	940	940	940	940	940	940
BAA					100	100	100	110	110	110	110	110
ICI	135	135	135	135	135	135	135	135	135	135	135	135
HendInGr	7350	7350	7350	7350	7350	7350	7350	7350	7350	7350	7350	7350
InvGrBrC	440	440	440	440	440	440	4400	4400	4400	4400	4400	4400
SPInvTr	5025	5025	5025	5025	5025	5025	5025	5025	5025	5025	5025	5025
MGCompGr	1686	1686	1686	1686	1686	1686	1686	1686	1686	1686	1686	1686
MGRec'y							1090	21800	21800	21800	21800	21800

Notes:

Number & scrip is the number of shares, defined as follows:

If purchased before 31/3/82, No & scr = total number on 31/3/82 plus scrip issue shares received since 31/3/82.

If purchased after 31/3/82, No & scr = number purchased in first tranche only, if purchased on more than one occasion, plus scrip issue shares received since purchase (attributable to shares in first tranche only). If some of these shares are sold partway through the review period, No & scr = the number held on the latest review date corrected back for scrip issues.

Table 13.3(b)

Company	31/03/82 Price/share	29/12/84	31/12/85	31/12/86	29/12/87	30/12/88	29/12/89	28/12/90	27/12/91	26/06/92	25/09/92	30/12/92
CommUn'n	141	185	230	266	333	340						
DavisServ					162	142	163	118	146	192	179	207
ICI												
MarksSp	155	120	176	179	182	151	201	223	271	333	327	328
SunServ	160	232	200	220								
Whitbread	107	216	250	263	268	300	391	443	411	435	450	494
BAA					95	260	381	415	523	676	715	789
ICI	318	736	756	1075	1075	1050	1134	874	1133	1222	1208	1056
HendInGr	49	96	120	148	160	172	215	179	183	197	195	216
InvGrBrC	110	211	238	287	296	327	42	34	40	43	42	46
SPInvTr	35	64	74	96	87	104	141	113	127	128	131	151
MGCompGr	174	298	338	426	448	521	658	556	600	679	655	732
MGRec'y							908	37	38	44	42	48

Notes:
Prices are in pence per share (or unit).
Prices for ordinary shares are middle market.
Prices for unit trusts are bid.

Table 13.3(c)

Company	31/03/82	29/12/84	31/12/85	31/12/86	29/12/87	30/12/88	29/12/89	28/12/90	27/12/91	26/06/92	25/09/92	30/12/92
	Price(cor'd)/share											
CommUn'n	141	185	230	266	333	340	463p					
DavisServ				174p	162	142	163	118	146	192	179	207
ICI												
MarksSp	78	120	176	179	182	151	201	223	271	333	327	328
SunServ	160	232	200	220	330p							
Whitbread	107	216	250	263	268	300	391	443	411	435	450	494
BAA				223	218	236	346	415	523	676	715	789
ICI	318	736	756	1075	1075	1050	1134	874	1133	1222	1208	1056
HendInGr	49	96	120	148	160	172	215	179	183	197	195	216
InvGrBrC	11	21	24	29	30	33	42	34	40	43	42	46
SPInvTr	35	64	74	96	87	104	141	113	127	128	131	151
MGCompGr	174	298	338	426	448	521	658	556	600	679	655	732
MGRec'y						50p	45	37	38	44	42	48
RPI	80.2	91.0	96.1	99.8	103.3	110.6	119.1	130.1	135.7	139.1	139.6	138.6
AlShl	323	590	682	833	891	926	1205	1038	1157	1224	1228	1358

Notes:

The *corrected price* of a share, Price(c), on a certain date, is the price, as recorded in the *Financial Times* for that date, corrected for any scrip issues which have been received in the review period.

$$\text{Price(c) (date x)} = \text{Price(date x)} \times \frac{\text{No. \& scrip(date x)}}{\text{No. \& scrip(30/12/92)}}$$

Purchase share prices are shown in currency format, i.e with the suffix 'p' in the date column which precedes the date of purchase. Sale share prices are shown in the date column which follows the date of sale.

Where payments for new issues are phased, the *corrected prices* are listed prices plus the outstanding payments; this means that the differences between the partially paid corrected prices and the fully paid prices are meaningful, although there is an advantage to the purchaser in having the payments phased, which this method of assessment does not recognise. The advantage is, of course, the fact that the money due for second phase payment can be earning interest in a bank, for instance, between the first and second phase payments.

In a takeover the shares are regarded as sold even when a share exchange occurs. The price is the cash equivalent offer. The calculated value of the shares being taken over then allows the equivalent purchase price of the shares in the taking over company to be calculated.

Purchase prices must also be corrected for scrip issues. The BAA purchase price, for instance, was 245p. There was a 1 for 10 scrip issue in 1990, however, so that the corrected purchase price is 222.7p.

The price of the BAA shares on 29/12/87 was 95p. On this date there was a phased payment of 145p still due. The corrected price is therefore:

$$= (95 + 145) \times 100/110$$
$$= 218p$$

Table 13.3(d)

Company	31/03/82 P/A ratio	29/12/84	31/12/85	31/12/86	29/12/87	30/12/88	29/12/89	28/12/90	27/12/91	26/06/92	25/09/92	30/12/92
CommUn'n	1.00											
DavisServ		0.72	0.77	0.73	0.86	0.84	0.88p.					
ICI				1.33p.	1.60	1.35	1.19	1.00	1.11	1.38	1.28	1.34
MarksSp	1.12	0.95	1.20	1.00	0.95	0.76	0.77	1.00	1.09	1.27	1.24	1.12
SunServ	2.29	1.81	1.35	1.22	1.33p.							
Whitbread	0.78	0.86	0.86	0.74	0.71	0.76	0.76	1.00	0.83	0.83	0.86	0.85
BAA				0.67p.	0.61	0.64	0.72	1.00	1.13	1.38	1.46	1.45
ICI	1.17	1.48	1.32	1.53	1.43	1.35	1.12	1.00	1.16	1.19	1.17	0.92
HendInGr	0.89	0.94	1.02	1.03	1.04	1.08	1.04	1.00	0.92	0.94	0.92	0.92
InvGrBrC	1.05	1.10	1.07	1.06	1.02	1.08	1.06	1.00	1.05	1.07	1.04	1.03
SPInvTr	1.00	1.00	0.99	1.05	0.89	1.03	1.07	1.00	1.01	0.96	0.97	1.02
MGCompGr	1.01	0.94	0.93	0.95	0.94	1.05	1.02	1.00	0.97	1.04	1.00	1.01
MGRec'y						1.17	1.06	1.00	0.93	1.01	0.96	1.00
AlShI	323	590	682	833	891	926	1205	1038	1157	1224	1228	1358

Notes:

P/A ratio = Price(c)/AlShI rebased to 1.0 on 28/12/90.

The ratios shown in currency format are calculated from the purchase (or sale) prices and the index on the day of purchase (or sale).

For shares sold before 28/12/90, the ratio price(c)/AlShI is rebased to 1.0 on 31/3/82 or the purchase date, whichever is the later.

The P/A ratio for DavisServ. shares is 1.33 on the date of the take-over. The rebasing constant for the SunServ. shares is calculated to give the same P/A ratio on the date of the takeover.

The P/A ratio of the UT(Acc) units (i.e. MGCompGr and MGRec'y) should increase faster than normal because the net dividends are reinvested. If the net yield is 3%, for instance, the P/A ratio should increase by 3% per annum, even though the price of the non-accummulation units only tracks the All Share Index.

Table 13.3(e)

Real gain, £.

Company		29/12/84	31/12/85	31/12/86	29/12/87	30/12/88	29/12/89	28/12/90	27/12/91	26/06/92	25/09/92	30/12/92
CommUn'n		570	1392	2064	3452	3319	5,782p.					
DavisServ					2996	1447	2123	−1042	196	2571	1814	3440
ICI												
MarksSp		385	998	991	986	529	1025	1167	1678	2383	2305	2329
SunServ		1486	244	616	3,739p.							
Whitbread		889	1145	1221	1224	1433	2182	2533	2162	2345	2479	2905
BAA					−33	−33	66	112	216	375	417	501
ICI		506	•	917	898	825	893	483	803	905	884	684
HendInGr		2921	4469	6338	7113	7627	10440	7271	7322	8211	8027	9579
InvGrBrC		378	466	659	678	772	1120	705	931	1040	986	1168
SPInvTr		1218	1588	2591	2087	2765	4436	2821	3385	3375	3480	4532
MGCompGr												
MGRec'y												
RPI	80.2	91.0	96.1	99.8	103.3	110.6	119.1	130.1	135.7	139.1	139.6	138.6

Notes:

Real gain,p. = Price(c) − Inflated price.

Real gain,£ = Real gain,p. × Number&Scrip / 100.

The inflated price is the corrected price on the start date, increased in line with the RPI.

$$\text{Infl price(date x)} = \text{StartPrice} \times \frac{\text{RPI(date x)}}{\text{RPI(start date)}}$$

For shares purchased before 31/3/82, the start date is 31/3/82. For shares purchased after 31/3/82, the start date and start price are the purchase date and price. For example, the figures for BAA are:

$$\text{Infl price (27/12/91)} = 222.7 \times 135.7 / 101.8 = 296.9\text{p}$$

where the BAA purchase price (corrected) was 222.7p and the RPI on the date of purchase was 101.8. Hence the real gain on 27/12/91 is:

$$\text{Real gain,p} = 523 − 296.9 = 226.1\text{p}$$

523p is the corrected share price on 27/12/91

$$\text{Real gain,£} = \text{Real gain,p} \times \text{No.\&Scrip} / 100 = 226.1 \times 110 = £ 248.7$$

Real gain of DavisServices shares calculated from Inflated Price of Sunlight Services shares, since DavisServ. shares were obtained in place of SunServ. shares, as a result of a take-over. This is in accordance with CGT law.

Suffix 'p.' indicates Real gain calculated from sale price and RPI on date of sale, rather than price and RPI on date at top of column.

Capital Gains Tax (CGT)

CGT payable on (real gain,£ − Exemption limit)

Above equation requires minor corrections for costs of sale, etc.

Exemption limit = £5800 in 1992/93.

The standard calculation of CGT is not suitable for UT(Acc) shares since the value of the share holding is partly a result of re-investing the dividends. For this reason the figures are omitted.

Table 13.3(f)

Company	P/E ratio	29/12/84	31/12/85	31/12/86	29/12/87	07/04/89	29/12/89	28/12/90	27/12/91	26/06/92	25/09/92	30/12/92
CommUn'n												
DavisServ		9.0	9.2	13.5	14.8	12.5	10.8	7.7	10.4	16.3	13.6	15.7
ICI												
MarkssSp		18.8	23.7	19.8	17.2	12.8	15.0	14.9	17.6	21.2	20.8	20.0
SunServ		16.8	9.4	11.9								
Whitbread		10.8	12.5	11.9	10.2	11.0	10.3	10.0	9.4	11.9	12.4	13.9
BAA					14.7	10.1	11.6	9.9	17.6	14.5	15.4	13.9
ICI		9.3	9.1	13.8	10.1	9.0	7.8	7.5	20.4	18.8	23.6	25.5
HendInGr												
InvGrBrC												
SPInvTr												
MGCompGr												
MGRec'y												

Notes:
The figures for the P/E ratio are abstracted from the *Financial Times* or some other newspaper.

Table 13.3(g)

% yield (gross)

Company	31/03/82	29/12/84	31/12/85	31/12/86	29/12/87	07/04/89	29/12/89	28/12/90	27/12/91	26/06/92	25/09/92	30/12/92
CommUn'n		9.1	7.3	6.2	5.3	6.7	4.8					
DavisServ					4.7	4.5	5.7	8.9	7.3	5.5	5.9	5.1
ICI												
MarksSp		3.7	2.8	3.1	3.4	4.3	3.7	3.8	3.3	2.8	2.9	2.9
SunServ		2.7	6.4	6.4								
Whitbread		4.1	4.0	4.2	4.2	4.0	4.3	4.5	5.3	5.2	5.0	4.6
BAA					3.8	4.6	3.1	3.7	3.3	2.9	2.7	2.5
ICI		4.7	5.7	4.3	5.7	5.7	5.9	8.4	6.5	6.0	6.1	6.9
HendInGr		3.8		3.4	2.8	4.2	4.0	6.3	5.7	5.0	4.8	4.3
InvGrBrC		3.2	3.1	2.5	3.4	2.1	4.0	3.3	3.1	1.8	2.3	1.8
SPInvTr		2.7	2.7	2.6	3.2	2.5	2.2	3.2	2.1	2.0	2.4	1.8
MGCompGr Reinve'd		3.3	3.8	3.3	3.1	3.0	3.9	6.9	4.8	4.2	4.3	3.6
MGRec'y Reinve'd		3.9	3.8	3.3	3.3	4.2	4.3	5.7	5.4	4.7	4.9	3.9
Average		4.1	4.4	3.9	3.9	4.2	4.2	5.5	4.7			3.7
Target	5.8	4.4	4.3	4.1	4.2	4.2	4.2	5.4	5.2			4.4

Notes:

The figures for the %yield (gross) are abstracted from the *Financial Times* or some other newspaper.

The % Yields (gross) for the accumulation units indicate the amount available for reinvestment, before the deduction of basic rate tax.

Table 13.3(h)

Company	*31/03/82*	*29/12/84*	*31/12/85*	*31/12/86*	*29/12/87*	*07/04/89*	*29/12/89*	*28/12/90*	*27/12/91*	*30/12/92*
		% Yield (net)								
CommUn'n					3.9	5.0				
DavisServ		6.4	5.1	4.4	3.4	3.4	4.3	6.7	5.5	3.8
ICI										
MarksSp		2.6	2.0	2.2	2.5	3.2	2.8	2.9	2.5	2.2
SunServ										
Whitbread		2.9	2.8	3.0	3.1	3.0	3.2	3.4	4.0	3.5
BAA					2.8	3.5	2.3	2.8	2.5	1.9
ICI		3.3	4.0	3.1	4.2	4.3	4.4	6.3	4.9	5.2
HendInGr		2.7		2.4	2.1	3.2	3.0	4.7	4.3	3.2
InvGrBrC		2.2	2.1	1.8	2.5	1.6	3.0	2.5	2.3	1.4
SPInvTr		1.9	1.9	1.8	2.3	1.9	1.7	2.4	1.6	1.4
MGCompGr ⎰ Rein-		2.3	2.7	2.3	2.2	2.3	2.9	5.2	3.6	2.7 ⎱ Rein-
MGRec'y ⎱ vested		2.7	2.6	2.3	2.4	3.2	3.2	4.3	4.1	2.9 ⎰ vested
Target	4.1	3.1	3.0	2.9	3.1	3.2	3.2	4.1	3.9	3.3
%Basic tax	30	30	30	29	27	25	25	25	25	25

Notes:

% Yield (net) = % Yield (gross) × (1 − % Tax / 100) where %Tax is the basic rate of tax.

The Real return could have been calculated from the % yield (gross) and the % tax, instead of the % yield (net), and in both cases the % real growth of course. Table 13.3(h) would not then have been required. The calculation would, however, have been more complicated, and the option of calculating the intermediate variable, the % yield (net) was preferred.

Table 13.3(i)

Company	31/03/82	29/12/84	31/12/85	31/12/86	29/12/87	30/12/88	29/12/89	28/12/90	27/12/91	30/12/92
		% Price growth to 30/12/92								
CommUn'n										
DavisServ					5.0	9.9	8.3	32.3	41.2	
ICI										
MarkSSp	14.4	13.4	9.3	10.6	12.5	21.4	17.8	21.2	20.8	
SunServ										
Whitbread	15.3	10.9	10.2	11.1	13.0	13.3	8.1	5.6	20.0	
BAA					29.3	35.1	31.5	37.7	50.2	
ICI	11.8	4.6	4.9	-0.3	-0.4	0.1	-2.3	9.9	-6.7	
HendInGr	14.7	10.7	8.7	6.5	6.1	5.8	0.0	9.7	17.5	
InvGrBrC	14.1	10.1	9.7	8.0	9.0	8.6	2.9	15.9	14.4	
SPInvTr	14.5	11.3	10.8	8.0	11.7	9.9	2.4	15.4	18.7	
MGCompGr	14.3	11.9	11.7	9.4	10.3	8.9	3.6	14.7	21.7	
MGRec'y							2.0	14.2	25.5	
RPI	80.2	91.0	96.1	99.8	103.3	110.6	119.1	130.1	135.7	138.6
AIShI	323	590	682	833	891	926	1205	1038	1157	1358
Period to 30/12/92										
Years	10.8	8.0	7.0	6.0	5.0	4.0	3.0	2.0	1.0	
% Infl/a	5.2	5.4	5.4	5.6	6.0	5.8	5.2	3.2	2.1	
% AIShI Growth/a	14.3	11.0	10.3	8.5	8.8	10.0	4.1	14.3	17.2	

Notes:

Definitions

'x' is date at top of column.

Years(x) are Years from date x to 30/12/92

%Infl/a = % Inflation per annum = RPI Growth/a.

ASI = AlShI = All Share Index

%ASIGr/a = % AlShI growth per annum.

%PrGr/a = % Price growth per annum.

%Infl/a = @Rate(RPI(30/12/92), RPI(x), Years(x))

%ASIGr/a = @Rate(ASI(30/12/92), ASI(x), Years(x)).

%PrGr/a = @Rate(Pr(30/12/92), Pr(x), Years(x))

By using more complicated equations it would have been possible to calculate the real growth directly from the corrected prices, the RPI and the dates. The Price Growth Table, 13.3(i), would not then have been required, nor would the rows devoted to the figures for Years and Inflation (intermediate variables). The advantage of calculating the intermediate variables is that it allows the cell addresses of the %Inflation and the Years to be used in the equations shown in the Notes for Table 13.3(i), rather than the equations for the %Inflation and the Years. In the same way the %AlShI growth and the %Inflation are used to calculate the %Target growth. It was decided that it was preferable to use the extra space to calculate the intermediate variables in order to keep the equations as simple as possible.

Table 13.3(j)

Company	31/03/82 % Real growth/annum to 30/12/92	29/12/84	31/12/85	31/12/86	29/12/87	30/12/88	29/12/89	28/12/90	27/12/91
CommUn'n									
DavisServ									
ICI					−1.0	3.9	2.9	28.2	38.3
MarksSp	8.7	7.6	3.7	4.7	6.1	14.7	12.0	17.4	18.3
SunServ									
Whitbread	9.6	5.2	4.6	5.2	6.5	7.1	2.8	2.3	17.5
BAA					21.9	27.7	25.0	33.4	47.1
ICI	6.3	−0.7	−0.5	−5.6	−6.0	−5.3	−7.1	6.5	−8.7
HendInGr	9.0	5.0	3.2	0.8	0.0	0.0	−4.9	6.3	15.1
InvGrBrC	8.5	4.5	4.1	2.3	2.8	2.7	−2.1	12.3	12.0
SPInvTr	8.8	5.6	5.1	2.2	5.3	3.9	−2.6	11.8	16.3
MGCompGr									
MGRec'y									
Target	8.6	5.3	4.7	2.7	2.6	4.0	−1.1	10.7	14.7

Notes:

Definitions

% Real growth/a = $100 \times (\text{PrGr/a} - \text{Infl/a})/(100 + \text{Infl/a})$

% Targ growth/a = $100 \times (\text{ASIGr/a} - \text{Infl/a})/(100 + \text{Infl/a})$

% Targ return/a = % Targ growth/a + Avg. % Targ yield(net)

For UT(Acc) shares the % Real growth/a. is the same as the % Real return/a.

M&G Compound Growth and M&G Recovery are UT(Acc) shares.

The standard of comparison for these unit trusts is therefore the % Targ return and not the % Targ growth. The Average Real growth is not therefore calculated because some of the shares are UT's and some UT(Acc)'s.

Table 13.3(k)

Company	31/03/82	29/12/84	31/12/85	31/12/86	29/12/87	30/12/88	29/12/89	28/12/90	27/12/91
			% Real return/annum to 30/12/92						
CommUn'n									
DavisServ					4	9	8	33	42
ICI									
MarksSp	11	10	6	7	9	17	14	20	20
SunServ									
Whitbread	13	8	8	9	10	11	6	6	21
BAA					24	30	27	36	49
ICI	11	4	4	−1	−1	0	−2	11	−3
HendInGr	12	8	6	4	4	4	−1	10	18
InvGrBrC	11	7	6	4	5	5	0	14	13
SPInvTr	11	7	7	4	7	6	−1	13	18
MGCompGr	8.6	6.1	6.0	3.6	4.0	2.9	−2	11.1	19.2
MGRec'y							−3.0	10.7	22.9
Average	11	7	6	5	7	9	5	17	22
Target	12	9	8	6	6	8	3	14	18

Notes:

For Ordinary shares and non-accumulation units, over the period from the date at the top of the column to the end date, i.e. 30/12/92:

$$\% \text{ Real return/a} = \% \text{ Real growth/a} + \text{average } \% \text{ Yield (net)}$$

For Accumulation unit trusts, over the period from the date at the top of the column to the end date, i.e. 30/12/92:

$$\% \text{ Real return / a} = \% \text{ Real growth / a}$$

The figures are recorded using the number of decimal places appropriate to the accuracy of the method of calculation.

Table 13.3(l)

Company		Period				% Growth/a.			
		From	To	Years	% Infl	Price	AlShI	Real	Target
CommUn'n	Sale	31/03/82	21/09/89	7.5	5.2	17.2	19.2	11.5	13.3
DavisServ	Purchase	08/07/87	30/12/92	5.5	5.8	3.2	3.2	-2.4	-2.5
ICI									
MarkssSp									
SunServ	Sale	31/03/82	08/07/87	5.3	4.6	14.7	27.1	9.6	21.5
Whitbread									
BAA	Purchase	21/07/87	30/12/92	5.4	5.8	26.1	2.3	19.2	-3.3
ICI									
HendInGr									
InvGrBrC									
SPInvTr									
MGCompGr									
MGRec'y	Purchase	21/09/89	30/12/92	3.3	5.3	-0.9	3.8	-5.9	

Also equal to % Real return/a
% Targ return = 2.2

Notes:

When the shares have been sold, the % Inflation, the Years and the % Real growth are counted from 31/3/82 to the date of sale.

When the shares were purchased after 31/3/82, the % Inflation, the Years and the % real growth are counted from the date of purchase to 30/12/92.

For Commercial Union and Sunlight Services, the Real and Target growth figures are for the periods from 31/3/82 to the date of sale.

For the Davis Services, BAA and M&G Recovery shares, the Real and Target growth figures are for the periods from the date of purchase to 30/12/92.

Table 13.4(c) Selected portfolio: performance (File: MspPort)

Company	82/83	83/84	84/85	85/86	86/87	87/88	88/89	89/90	90/91	91/92	92/93
	Net dividend, pence/share										
CommUn'n	11.8	11.8	11.8	11.8	12.15	13.45	17.00	19.90			
DavisSer						8.60	6.33	7.27	7.98	7.98	7.98
ICI	19.00	24.00	30.00	33.00	36.00	41.00	43.00				
MarksSp	2.35	2.65	3.18	3.57	4.05	4.65	5.25	5.75	6.55	6.80	7.20
SunServ	3.52	4.84	7.18	8.22	10.95						
Whitbr A	5.05	7.15	7.15	7.15	8.05	9.20	11.00	13.10	15.30	16.55	17.15
BAA						3.00	7.75	10.00	12.25	13.50	15.00
ICI	19.00	24.00	30.00	33.00	36.00	41.00	43.00	53.00	55.00	55.00	55.00
HendInGr	2.61	3.35	3.56	3.96	4.48	5.06	5.97	7.26	9.04	9.88	9.96
InvGrBrC	2.15	4.26	5.05	6.01	5.99	6.95	6.95	0.92	1.42	1.05	1.10
SPInvTr	1.37	1.43	1.50	1.60	1.75	1.90	2.18	2.38	3.29	2.91	2.46
MGCompGr	4.80	5.34	5.48	7.58	8.75	10.64	10.90	12.36	21.16	20.41	19.97
MGRec'y								9.50	1.52	1.62	1.32

Notes:

Table 13.4(a) Total number
  The total number of shares held by a single owner in each company.

Table 13.4(b) Price / share

Tables 13.4(a) and 13.4(b) are not printed for the reasons given in the notes appended to Table 13.4(f). The figures are recorded on the floppy disk.

The figures in Table 13.4(c) are the total dividends paid during the tax year. Each figure is normally the sum of the interim and final dividend. The figures are obtained from the dividend warrants (tax vouchers). By moving the pointer to the appropriate cell in Table 13.4(c) on the floppy disk, the individual dividends will be shown in the control panel.

Table 13.4(d)

Company	82/83 Net dividend,£	83/84	84/85	85/86	86/87	87/88	88/89	89/90	90/91	91/92	92/93
CommUn'n	269.04	269.48	269.04	269.04	277.02	312.89	396.95	464.67			
DavisSer						117.53	354.29	406.90	446.64	446.64	446.65
ICI	21.28	26.88	33.60	36.96	40.32	45.92	48.18	1.99			
MarksSp	28.20	31.80	38.16	42.84	48.60	55.80	63.00	69.00	78.60	82.28	87.17
SunServ	103.84	142.53	211.53	242.16	322.59	191.49					
Whitbr A	47.47	52.64	60.63	67.21	75.67	86.48	103.40	123.14	143.82	155.57	161.21
BAA						3.00	7.75	10.00	12.77	14.85	16.49
ICI	25.65	32.40	40.50	44.55	48.60	55.35	58.05	130.91	135.85	135.85	135.85
HendInGr	191.99	246.02	261.60	291.41	328.97	371.61	438.82	533.87	661.12	726.02	733.24
InvGrBrC	9.46	18.75	22.22	26.44	26.37	30.58	42.90	40.50	62.33	46.02	48.35
SPInvTr	68.84	71.85	75.37	80.39	87.93	95.47	109.54	119.58	165.31	146.22	123.61
MGCompGr	80.93	90.10	92.46	127.77	147.44	179.46	183.72	208.32	356.76	344.06	336.71
MGRec'y								103.55	330.71	353.38	287.98
Total	846.70	982.45	1105.11	1228.77	1403.51	1545.58	1806.60	2212.43	2393.91	2450.89	2377.26

Notes:

The net dividend,£ figures are abstracted from the dividend warrants. They are normally the sum of the interim and the final dividends paid in the tax year. The information in this table is useful for tax reporting purposes.

As a cross check, the number of shares multiplied by the net dividend per share should equal the net dividend,£.

The dividends for the UT(Acc.) shares are reinvested, not distributed; i.e MGCompGr and MGRec'y.

The gross dividend can be calculated from the net dividend by using the following equation:

$$\text{Gross dividend} = \text{Net dividend} / (1 - \%\,\text{Tax} / 100)$$

where % Tax is the Basic rate of tax.

Table 13.4(e)

Company	84/85 Yield % (net)	85/86	86/87	87/88	88/89	89/90	90/91	91/92	92/93
CommUn'n	6.38	5.13	4.57	4.04	5.00	4.30			
DavisSer				5.31	4.46	4.46	6.76	5.47	
ICI	4.08	4.37	3.35	3.81	4.10				
MarksSp	2.65	2.03	2.26	2.55	3.48	2.87	2.94	2.51	2.20
SunServ	3.09	4.11	4.98						
Whitbr A	3.31	2.86	3.06	3.43	3.67	3.35	3.45	4.03	3.47
BAA				3.16	2.98	2.62	2.95	2.58	1.90
ICI	4.08	4.37	3.35	3.81	4.10	4.67	6.29	4.85	5.21
HendInGr	3.72	3.30	3.03	3.15	3.47	3.37	5.05	5.39	4.62
InvGrBrC	2.39	2.52	2.09	2.35	2.98	2.20	4.19	2.63	2.41
SPInvTr	2.33	2.16	1.83	2.18	2.10	1.69	2.90	2.29	1.63
MGCompGr	1.84	2.24	2.06	2.37	2.09	1.88	3.81	3.40	2.73
MGRec'y							4.11	4.23	2.74
Total	3.39	3.34	3.20	3.07	3.46	3.45	4.45	4.17	3.30

Notes:

% Yield (net) = Divi (net) / Value at end Dec. × 100

For the total portfolio (see Table 13.4(f)), the Yield (net) is calculated from the sum of the net divi's paid in the tax year, divided by the portfolio value at the end of December.

The dividends were totalled over the tax year, because these figures are required anyway for the investor's tax returns.

A more rigorous treatment would divide the net dividend over the past year by the average portfolio value over the same period.

Table 13.4(f)

Company	31/03/82 Value,£	29/12/84	31/12/85	31/12/86	29/12/87	30/12/88	29/12/89	28/12/90	27/12/91	30/12/92
CommUn'n	3215	4218	5244	6065	7776	7939	9123	6604	8172	11586
DavisSer					9067	7948				
ICI	356	824	847	1204	1204	1176				
MarksSp	930	1440	2112	2148	2184	1812	2406	2676	3279	3969
SunServ	4714	6835	5892	6481						
Whitbr A	1006	2030	2350	2472	2519	2820	3675	4164	3863	4644
BAA					95	260	381	457	575	868
ICI	429	994	1021	1451	1451	1418	2801	2159	2799	2608
HendInGr	3631	7041	8820	10856	11789	12635	15832	13161	13465	15854
InvGrBrC	485	928	1047	1263	1303	1441	1840	1491	1751	2006
SPInvTr	1774	3231	3713	4799	4371	5211	7070	5698	6386	7597
MGCompGr	2940	5028	5697	7176	7560	8781	11096	9374	10113	12338
MGRec'y							9894	8044	8349	10508
Total	19480	32569	36743	43914	49320	51439	64117	53828	58753	71978

Notes:

The equation used to calculate the value of each share holding is as follows:

$$\text{Value}, £ = \text{Number} \times \text{Price} / \text{share} / 100$$

The total value of the portfolio is simply the sum of the values of the individual holdings.

Table 13.4(a) records the total number of shares held in each company. To conserve space, this Table has not been printed. The numbers can be derived from Table 13.2. The total number of shares is equal to the 'Number & Scrip', plus any shares purchased minus any sold, after the purchase of the first tranche.

Table 13.4(b) containing the price/share data, is not printed, since the figures are identical to those in Table 13.3(b).

	31/03/82	29/12/84	31/12/85	31/12/86	29/12/87	30/12/88	29/12/89	28/12/90	27/12/91	30/12/92
Port value,£	19480	32569	36743	43914	49320	51439	64117	53828	58753	71978
Invested,£	19480	199	128	152	444	329	208	687	721	625
InvFract,£		135	87	103	274	221	142	450	478	410
Performance criteria										
Past year										
% Real gr/a		14.9	6.4	14.6	7.5	-3.2	15.3	-24.0	3.3	18.8
% Targ gr/a		18.9	9.5	17.6	3.3	-2.9	20.8	-21.1	6.8	14.9
% yield (net)										
Portfolio		3.4	3.3	3.2	3.1	3.5	3.5	4.4	4.2	3.3
Target		3.1	3.0	2.9	3.1	3.5	3.2	4.1	3.9	3.3
Period to 30/12/92										
% Real gr/a	6.5	3.7	3.6	1.9	0.8	1.9	-2.2	10.9	18.8	
% Targ gr/a	8.6	5.3	4.7	2.7	2.6	4.0	-1.1	10.8	14.7	
% Real ret/a		7	7	6	5	6	2	15	22	
% Targ ret/a		9	8	6	6	8	3	14	18	
Intermediate variables										
Past year										
% Growth/a										
Port Val		20.3	12.4	19.1	11.2	3.6	24.2	-17.0	7.7	21.3
Infl		4.7	5.6	3.9	3.5	7.1	7.7	9.2	4.3	2.1
AIShI		24.5	15.6	22.1	7.0	3.9	30.1	-13.8	11.4	17.4
Period to 30/12/92								Trial%		
Years	10.8	8.0	7.0	6.0	5.0	4.0	3.0	2.0	1.0	21.3
Trial val	19480	26916	30311	34143	38752	43797	49322	56031	63590	71959
Trial val	19480	32569	36743	43914	49320	51439	64117	53828	58753	71979
% Growth/a										
Port val	12.1	9.3	9.2	7.6	6.9	7.8	2.9	14.4	21.3	
Infl	5.2	5.4	5.4	5.6	6.0	5.8	5.2	3.2	2.1	
AIShI	14.3	11.0	10.3	8.5	8.8	10.0	4.1	14.3	17.2	
RPI	80.2	91.0	96.1	99.8	103.3	110.6	119.1	130.1	135.70	138.60
AIShI	322.7	590.0	682.0	833.0	891.0	926.0	1205.0	1038.4	1157.10	1358.10
% Tax (basic)	30	30	29	27	25	25	25	25	25	25

Notes (Table 13.4(g)):
Data to be transferred to Table 13.4:
   Invested and Invested Fraction from Table 13.2.
   RPI, AlShI and % Basic Tax from Table 13.3.

The yield (net) of the portfolio is from Table 13.4(e).

Calculation of performance criteria over past year:

   Calculate the % Growth/annum for portfolio value
   (Port), Inflation and AlShI, for Past year and Period to 30/12/92.

% Growth/a. (Gr) of Port over the past year is:
   $=100\times(Port(x+1)-Port(x)-Inv)/(Port(x)+InvFrac)$
   where x and x+1 are two dates one year apart.

   Example: %Growth/a. on 31/12/85, for the Past year, i.e. for 1985, is:
   $= 100\times(36743-32569-128)/(32569+87) = 12.4\%$ p.a.

Calculation of performance criteria over full review period:

   Calculate %Growth/a for RPI and AlShI for periods to 30/12/92

Calculation of % Growth/a (Gr) of Port to 30/12/92, using the trial and error method:

   $Port(x+1) = Port(x)+Inv+Gr/100\times(Port(x)+InvFrac)$

Example: Calculation of trial values for Port growth rate over full period of review (top trial row).

   Try Gr = 10%. Then compare trial value on 30/12/92 with portfolio value on this date. After one or two more trials, correct figure of 12.1 % is arrived at.

The calculations for two of the annual periods between 31/3/82 and 30/12/92 are shown below:

   Trial value(31/12/85)
   $= 26916+128+12.1/100\times(26916+87) = £30311$
   Repeat until Trial value (30/12/92)
   $= 63590+625+12.1/100\times(63590+410) = £71959$
   £71959 is near enough to £71978 to decide that no further trial is required and 12.1 % is correct.

The figure on 29/12/84, £26916, is calculated from

   $=19480\times(1+12.1/100\times9/12)\times(1+12.1/100)\times(1+12.1/100)+199(1+12.1/100\times0.7)$

This is an approximation, but accurate enough.

Calculation of Performance criteria over range of periods, all ending on 30/12/92;

Intermediate growth rates are calculated on the second trial row. To calculate %Growth/a from 29/12/84 enter portfolio value as start value in trial row (£32569). Calculate trial values in subsequent years using same equations as for first row.

Second Trial val row in the Table shows the last Growth calculation on this row, i.e. from 27/12/91,

$$58753 + 21.3 / 100 \times 58753 = 71979$$

This is very close to 71978 and confirms that the growth rate of 21.3 % p.a. is correct, for the Port value for the last year of the review period.

Calculate %Real growth/a, %Target growth/a, %Real return/a and % Target return/a for past year and period to 30/12/92.

% Real growth/a = 100 × (PortGr-Infl) / (100+Infl)
% Targ growth/a = 100 × (AlShIGr-Infl) / (100+Infl)
% Real return/a = %Real growth/a. + % Yield (net)

where % Yield (net) is the average net yield over the years to 30/12/92.

For Target yield and Target return, see Chapter 10 and Table 13.3.

Table 13.4(h) Real return (IRR method)

	31/03/82	29/12/84	31/12/85	31/12/86	29/12/87	30/12/88	29/12/89	28/12/90	27/12/91	30/12/92
Port value,£	19480	32569	36743	43914	49320	51439	64117	53828	58753	71978
Past year										
Invested,£			128	152	444	329	208	687	721	625
Net divi,£			1229	1404	1512	1779	2212	2394	2451	2377
Port yield,%		3.4	3.3	3.2	3.1	3.5	3.5	4.4	4.2	3.3
Targ yield,%		3.1	3.0	2.9	3.1	3.5	3.2	4.1	3.9	3.3
Performance criteria.										
Period to 30/12/92										
%Real ret/a		8	8	6	5	6	1	15	23	
%Targ ret/a		9	8	6	6	8	3	14	18	
Period to 30/12/92										
Cash flow,£		−32569	1101	1252	1067	1450	2004	1706	1730	73730
Cash fl (IRR)		−32569	−36743	−43914	−49320	−51439	−64117	−53828	−58753	73730
% IRR									25.5	
% Return/a		13.7	13.3	11.6	10.9	11.9	6.5	18.7	25.5	
Years		8.0	7.0	6.0	5.0	4.0	3.0	2.0	1.0	
%Infl/a		5.4	5.4	5.6	6.0	5.8	5.2	3.2	2.1	
%AlShI gr/a		11.0	10.3	8.5	8.8	10.0	4.1	14.3	17.2	
%AlShI ret/a		14.3	13.8	12.0	12.4	13.7	7.8	17.9	20.5	

Notes:

Transfer 'Invested' figures from Table 13.2.
Transfer RPI and AIShI figures from Table 13.3.
Transfer 'NetDividend,£' figures from Table 13.4(c).

Calculate % Inflation/a, % AIShI Growth/a, %target yield and %target return/a using the methods shown in Tables 13.1 or 13.3.

Calculate figures for cash flow:
For the years between the first and last of the review period:

$$\text{Cash Flow} = \text{Net dividend} - \text{Invested}$$

For the first year:

$$\text{Cash Flow} = - \text{portfolio value}$$

For the last year:

$$\text{Cash Flow} = \text{Port value} + \text{Net divi} - \text{Invested}$$

Use the Lotus function @IRR to calculate the % Returns for the range of periods, all starting at the date at the top of the Table and finishing at the end date.

There are two lines allocated to cash flow. First is the cash flow for the full period of the review, i.e. 29/12/84 to 30/12/92. The second, called Cash Fl(IRR), to distinguish it from the first line of cash flow figures, is for use in calculating the % Return/a. figures, for the intermediate periods, e.g. 31/12/85 to 30/12/92, 31/12/86 to 30/12/92, etc. More examples are given on the floppy disk in the Computer Tips section. The results of the @IRR calculation are produced in the % IRR line. The value is then copied to the % Return/a line as a permanent record, since the figure in the % IRR line will alter as the calculations for the later time periods are carried out.

$$\% \text{ Return/a.} = @\text{IRR}(\text{Guess No., Range of Cash Flows})$$

For the period 29/12/84 to the end date, 30/12/92, for example:

$$\% \text{ Return/a} = @\text{IRR}(10\%, 32569..73730)) = 13.7$$

For the period 31/12/85 to the end date, 30/12/92, for example:

$$\% \text{ Return/a} = @\text{IRR}(10\%, 36743..73730)) = 13.3 \%$$

APPENDIX 1

How to put the System into use

GENERAL

This Appendix outlines the actions needed to put the System into use. This in effect means constructing the equivalent of Tables 13.2, 13.3 and 13.4 for the investor's own shares. Chapter 9 provided a general picture of the contents of the files. The list of actions which follow will make reference to the chapter and/or appendix in which information can be found on the part of the System being put into use. Reference will also be made to the table where the System has been applied to the *selected portfolio*. Readers can consult the table either in the printed form or on the computer disk, although it should be noted that the growth and return figures are measured over different periods. The equations, formulae or functions used in the calculations, that are needed to construct the tables, are appended to the printed table in which they have been used. They can be found on the disk in the control panel whenever the cell pointer is positioned on a cell which contains the result of a calculation.

Readers can construct a table for their own investment data and performance criteria either by copying the headings/labels and equations, etc., from the printed *selected portfolio* tables or by entering their own data in place of, or in addition to the *selected portfolio* data on a copy of the disk supplied with this book. This latter option avoids most of the work involved in entering the headings and constructing the equations, etc. The notes which follow do not attempt to distinguish between these two approaches. The main steps in the construction of the three files for the equity shares are as follows:

1 Open a file with the title '*MspData*' – (Appendix 1).
   Enter Headings – (Table 13.2).
   Enter data for share holdings – (Table 13.2).
   Carry out the required calculations – (Chapter 6 and Table 13.2).

2 Open a file with the title '*MspPri*' – (Appendix 1).
Enter Headings – (Table 13.3).
Transfer the following figures from File '*MspData*':
No & scrip, – (Appendix 1).
Enter data, and in particular share prices for equity shares, RPI
and AlShI – (Chapter 5 and Table 13.3).
Carry out the required calculations – (Chapter 5, Appendix 1 and
Table 13.3).
Produce summary, if required, of each share's performance –
(Chapter 11).

3 Open a file with the title '*MspPort*' – (Appendix 1).
Enter Headings – (Table 13.4).
Transfer the following figures from file '*MspData*':
Number, Invested, Invested fraction, – (Appendix 1).
Transfer share prices, RPI and AlShI from '*MspPri*' file.
Enter other data (e.g. dividends),
Carry out the required calculations – (Chapter 6, Appendix 1 and
Table 13.4).
Produce summary of portfolio performance – (Chapter 11).

4 Open a file with the title '*MspFIInv*' – (Appendix 1).
Enter headings – (Appendix 1).
Transfer company names, Invested and Invested fraction from the
file '*MspData*'.
Transfer the RPI figures from the *MspPri* file.
Enter Number, Dividend and Price/share.
Carry out the required calculations – (Chapter 12 and Appendix 1).

Each of the four files mentioned above is discussed in sufficient detail
in the following sections to allow the reader to construct them on their
own computer. Readers are reminded that some of the data recommended for collection in these files is not included in the files for the
selected portfolio shown in the printed Tables 13.2, 13.3 and 13.4,
such data having no general relevance. An example of such data is the
identification number on the share certificates, which has no meaning
to the reader, but which is important to the investor who owns the

shares. As is seen, there is a fair amount of work involved in putting the System into use. Once the files have been constructed, however, the work required to update the data in the files is minimal, unless a high frequency of data entry and calculation is chosen. Prices, dividend data, P/E ratios, changes in the portfolio and the indices are entered, a limited amount of data is transferred from one file to another and then the calculations are carried out. The computer copying facility allows the calculations to be carried out easily and quickly, once the equations or functions have been entered.

MEASURING SHARE PERFORMANCE – DATA

This section describes how the *MspData* file is constructed.

All the labels or headings can be seen in Table 13.2, which shows the *MspData* file for the *selected portfolio*, either in print or on the disk. The vertical-axis labels of this file consist firstly of the names of the companies whose investments are held, arranged in categories. The categories of investments were defined in Table 6.1. The shares of each owner are grouped together within each category, unless a portfolio performance is required for each owner. The Peps are analysed separately because some of the information needed to carry out the analysis is not always available, e.g. valuations are generally only provided by the managers once or twice a year. Following the names of the companies/shares in each category there comes the Label 'Total'.

The following data is not included in the printed Table 13.2 for the *selected portfolio*, but should be included in the file constructed by private investors for their own portfolio.

Certificates	Share no.	Number of shares
	Cert. No.	No. on certificate
	Date	Date on certificate
	Nom val	Nominal value/share

Some of the sub-headings can be repeated as often as required. This is necessary when, for instance, there is more than one scrip issue, or dividends are repeatedly reinvested in the same company's shares.

When purchasing some shares, the payments are phased. In such a case, under the 'Purchased' heading, the first two headings record the total number of shares purchased and the total price per share. The next four columns are repeated as often as is necessary to record each of the phased payments.

The purchase of extra shares is sometimes the result of the investor taking up the opportunity to reinvest the dividend, and the 'Extra Purchased' columns in the file are designed for small investments of this kind. If a major investment is made in a company's shares which are already held, however, it would be necessary to add two more columns to allow the AlShI and the RPI to be recorded.

The range of dates chosen for the headings 'Invested' and 'Invested Fraction' is a matter for personal choice. The System assumes a minimum data entry frequency of quarterly.

The following expenditures or receipts are recorded under the 'Invested' headings:

Expenditures (Positive sign)
Cost of purchasing shares
Value of dividend reinvested in purchasing shares
Value of dividend reinvested in unit trust(Acc) units

Receipts (Negative sign)
Received from sale of shares
Received when Rights Issue not taken up

When shares are held in a company which is taken over and they are replaced with shares in the taking-over company the original shares are valued at the cash offer. This allows the transaction to be treated as a sale which occurs simultaneously with a purchase, the revenue and expenditure being equal.

MEASURING SHARE PERFORMANCE – PRICES

The second file is the *MspPri* file, which allows the performance criteria *price ratio, real gain, real growth* and *real return* of each share to be calculated, together with the target figures, over the chosen period of time and at the chosen frequency. An example of the use of an *MspPri* file can be seen in Table 13.3 for the *selected portfolio*. The first 65 lines of the spreadsheet are devoted to the recording / calculating of the basic data, i.e. the number of shares, the share price and the corrected price, and also the short-term criteria, i.e. the *P/A ratio, real gain*, P/E ratio and the gross yield. The first group of vertical headings (labels) list the companies in which shares are held, in order of category, and then the labels 'Average' and 'Target' followed by the indices, RPI and AlShI.

The next 65 lines of the spreadsheet are devoted to the recording and calculating of the medium and long-term criteria, the *real growth* and the *real return*. The frequency of data entry would normally be lower than for the short-term criteria. The yield (net) is first of all calculated from the yield (gross) and the %tax (Basic), and then the price growth is calculated. The yield (net) and the price growth are intermediate variables, calculated so that the equations needed to calculate the *real growth* and the *real return* are simpler. The years, inflation/a and AlShIgrowth/a. are also intermediate variables and are calculated for the same reason.

The vertical headings are as follows:

Company Names

Average
Target

Indices
  RPI
  AlShI
% Basic Tax
Period to end review date
  Years
  %Infl/a.
  %AlShI Growth/a.

The System of performance monitoring described so far has been concerned solely with the performance of the shares already owned by the investor. The parts of the System concerned with individual shares can also be used to monitor the performance of shares not at present owned, but under consideration for purchase. This can be achieved by inserting some further labels, below the company names on the vertical axis. These extra labels are simply the names of the companies whose shares the investor is considering buying. The prices can then be entered and the *P/A ratio*, and perhaps even the growth rates, calculated in the same way as for the shares already owned. The investor will probably also want to record the yield and P/E ratio.

Purchase and sale prices and calculations based on these prices are entered in this file in currency format, i.e. the figure is followed by the letter 'p.', as explained in Chapter 5.

The table should be designed to allow frequent entry of share prices and also the calculation and recording of the corrected prices, the *P/A ratio* and the *real gain*, since these are the criteria recommended as part of the System for monitoring the short-term performance of shares. After a period of perhaps six months or a year many of these prices can be erased. The dividend cover is not included, because it can be calculated from the yield and the P/E ratio. Nevertheless some investors may choose to include it for convenience.

MEASURING SHARE PERFORMANCE – PORTFOLIOS

The third file, '*MspPort*' , contains the data needed to assess the performance of a portfolio of shares. Table 13.4 shows the use of this file for the *selected portfolio*. Lines 1 to 65 of the spreadsheet are devoted to the recording / calculation of the total number, price/ share, net dividend (pence/share), net dividend,£, net dividend yield and the value,£, ovor a range of dates, for each of the shares in the *selected portfolio*.

The next 65 lines of the spreadsheet are devoted to the calculation of the *real growth*, by the direct (T&E) method, and from this the *real return*. The first line records the portfolio value, the figures being transferred from the totals of the columns with the title 'Value', in lines 1 to 65. The order of calculation is not the same as the order of the vertical headings, because the latter are arranged for convenience of reading and interpretation, rather than in calculation order. The *real growths, target growths, real returns* and *target returns*, i.e. the criteria needed to assess the performance of the portfolio, are therefore placed below the figures for the portfolio values. Further down the table are the basic data and the intermediate variables, such as the growth rates, which are needed to calculate the performance criteria.

The next 65 lines of the spreadsheet are devoted to the calculation of the *real return p.a.*, by the direct (IRR) method, and from this the *real growth p.a.* Again the first line records the portfolio value.

MEASURING SHARE PERFORMANCE – FIXED INTEREST INVESTMENTS

The basic data for the fixed interest investments are recorded, together with the data for equities, in the *MspData* file, whilst the performance of these investments is assessed in the *MspFIInv* file. The construction of this file is the same as that of the *MspPri* file, without the calculation of the growth and *real growth* for each share. The figures for yield have to be calculated from the stock price and the % interest or coupon, or dividend paid, rather than being abstracted from the newspaper, as was the case for the shares in the *MspPri* file.

As was the case for equities, for tax reporting reasons the dividends are classified according to owner; they are also classified according to the tax regime to which they have been subjected, i.e. tax credit, income tax or nil tax deducted.

The horizontal headings or labels are shown in Table A1.1. The number total, price/share, etc. each have a number of columns, one for each date chosen for data entry. The frequency with which data are entered is a matter for individual choice, and is discussed in more detail in Chapter 9.

This file combines the duties of the *MspPri* and *MspPort* files, but for fixed interest investments instead of equities. This is possible because the space taken up by the *corrected price*, *P/A ratio*, P/E ratio, *real gain*, price growth and *real growth* columns is not required

Table A1.1 MspFIInv file – headings – horizontal axis

Company	Issuer of shares, loans, etc.	
Interest paid	Nom.%	
Date	Red'n	Redemption
Date	Conv'n	Conversion
Tax	Tax Credit, Income Tax or Nil Tax.	
Number total	31/3/82 to 30/12/92	Total number of shares, units,etc.
Price/share pence	31/3/82 to 30/12/92	
Divi/share pence	82/83 to 91/92	
Dividend,£	82/83 to 91/92	Net of tax
Net yield %	82/83 to 91/92	100 × Net divi / price both in pence / share.
Real return % p.a.	31/3/82 to 30/12/92	See Chapter 5
Redemption yield	Date %GrYield	Yield to redemption
Value ,£	31/3/82 to 30/12/92	Number × Price/share

for fixed interest investments. The most important information produced in the *MspFIInv* file is the data on *real return* for the individual investments and for the portfolio, the latter being calculated by the IRR method.

APPENDIX 2

Share performance – derivation of equations

This appendix is included for those readers who are interested in the way in which the equations used in Chapter 5 have been derived. This understanding will allow such readers to tailor-make the performance measurement System to suit their own particular needs.

GROWTH OVER PAST YEAR

The way in which the *real growth* and *targ growth* of a share can be calculated was described in Chapter 5. The theoretical basis for the calculations is now outlined.

The standard definition of the growth of a range of values over a range of dates, is as follows:

$$\% \text{ Growth} = (\text{Value}(y) - \text{Value}(x)) \times 100 / \text{Value}(x)$$

Value(x) is the value on date x, and Value(y) is the value on date y, date x preceding date y. When x and y are one year apart, the *%Growth* becomes the *%Growth/a*.

Hence:

$$\% \text{ Price growth} = (\text{Price}(y) - \text{Price}(x)) \times 100 / \text{Price}(x),$$
$$\text{i.e. PrGr} / 100 = \text{Pr}(y) / \text{Pr}(x) - 1.0$$
$$\text{where Pr} = \text{Price and PrGr} = \% \text{ Price growth};$$
$$\text{i.e. Pr}(y) / \text{Pr}(x) = \text{PrGr} / 100 + 1.0 \qquad \text{[Equation 1]}$$

The equivalent equations can be derived for the range of RPI and AlShI figures:

$$\text{RPIGr} = (\text{RPI}(y) - \text{RPI}(x)) \times 100 / \text{RPI}(x)$$

The RPI growth rate (RPIGr) is more commonly known as the rate of inflation (Infl). Hence:

$$\text{Infl} = (\text{RPI}(y) - \text{RPI}(x)) \times 100 / \text{RPI}(x)$$

i.e.

$$\text{RPI}(y) / \text{RPI}(x) = \text{Infl} / 100 + 1 \qquad \text{[Equation 2]}$$

In the same way, the % AlShI growth (AlShIGr) can be calculated:

$$\text{AlShIGr} = (\text{AlShI}(y) - \text{AlShI}(x)) \times 100 / \text{AlShI}(x)$$

The *real growth* is defined as the increase in the price of the share at constant prices (cost of living prices, not share prices, of course), divided by the price, times 100. The quantitative development of this concept can be expressed as follows:

$$\text{Increase in share price} = \text{Pr}(y) - \text{Pr}(x)$$

In terms of the purchasing power of the £ on date x, the share price on date y is worth $\text{Pr}(y) \times \text{RPI}(x) / \text{RPI}(y)$. Hence:

$$\text{Increase(constant prices)} = \text{Pr}(y) \times \text{RPI}(x) / \text{RPI}(y) - \text{Pr}(x)$$

Therefore:

$$\%real\ growth = (\text{Pr}(y) \times \text{RPI}(x) / \text{RPI}(y) - \text{Pr}(x)) \times 100 / \text{Pr}(x)$$
$$\text{i.e. RealGr} = (\text{Pr}(y) / \text{Pr}(x) \times \text{RPI}(x) / \text{RPI}(y) - 1.0) \times 100$$

Substituting Equation 1 in the above equation:

$$\text{RealGr} = ((\text{PrGr}/100 + 1.0) \times \text{RPI}(x)/\text{RPI}(y) - 1.0) \times 100$$
$$= (\text{PrGr} + 100) \times \text{RPI}(x)/\text{RPI}(y) - 100$$

Substituting Equation 2 in the above equation:

$$\text{RealGr} = ((\text{PrGr} + 100) \times 100 / (\text{Infl} + 100)) - 100$$
$$= ((\text{PrGr} + 100) - (\text{Infl} + 100)) \times 100 / (\text{Infl} + 100)$$
$$= 100 \times (\text{PrGr} - \text{Infl}) / (100 + \text{Infl})$$

$$\text{[Equation 3]}$$

The *target growth* (TargGr) is the *real growth* that would have been achieved if the share price had tracked the All Share Index. By definition, therefore, the AlShI growth rate is substituted for the

Price growth rate to calculate the Target growth rate. Hence:

% TargGr = 100 × (AlShIGr − Infl) / (100 + Infl)

[Equation 4].

The *% target growth* is therefore independent of the share price, being a function of only the All Share Index and the Retail Price Index. This means that the *target growth* provides a common objective or target for all equity shares. The fact that the *target growth* is independent of share prices is a major advantage of the System, resulting in a considerable saving in space and calculation, and also making the assessment of performance easier to understand. It means that the *target growth* is a common target for all shares and portfolios. This is a deliberate consequence of the way in which the *real* and *target growths* are defined. Figure 4.2 shows how these concepts can be expressed graphically.

THE GROWTH RATE OVER A PERIOD OF YEARS

The equations outlined above can be used without modification to calculate the different growth rates when the period between x and y is one year. They are therefore available for use in the System to calculate the growth rates over the past year. The preferred method of assessment of share price performance, however, is the growth rate from the date at the top of the column to the end of the review period.

At first sight this growth rate can be calculated from the price on date x (say 200), the price at the end-date (say 320) and the intervening years (say three), as follows:

% Growth = (320 − 200) × 100 / 200 = 60 %
and % Growth/a = 60 / 3 = 20 % per annum

This calculation gives the simple rate of growth, whereas the compound rate is more meaningful and has been assumed in the calculations used in the System. It can be considered to be the annual rate of interest that would have to be earned in order for the share price to grow to 320 at the end of three years. The interest would be added at the end of each year and there would be no withdrawals. The compound rate of growth (PrGr) is defined by the following calculation:

Start price = 200
Price after 1 year = 200 × (1.0 + PrGr/100)
Price after 2 years
= 200 × (1.0 + PrGr/100) × (1.0 + PrGr/100)
Price after 3 years
= 200 × (1.0 + PrGr/100) × (1.0 + PrGr/100) × (1.0 + PrGr/100)
= 320
since the price after 3 years has been stated to be 320.

The *%Growth/a* can be obtained by solving this equation. This can be accomplished in three ways.

Firstly, different figures for the growth rate can be used in the equation, the correct growth rate being the one for which the equation gives the value of 320. This is called the trial and error method.

Secondly, compound interest tables are available which give the growth rate when the start price, end price and years are known.

Thirdly, most spreadsheets contain formulae/functions for solving compound growth (or interest) equations. The function in the Lotus Spreadsheet is:

@RATE(End Price,Start Price,Years)

This facility is much the best and is assumed to be available in the System.

The compound growth rate in the above example is 17.0 per cent per annum. incidentally, compared with the simple growth rate of 20 per cent per annum. The difference between the two rates can be much larger than this when either the time period and/or the rate of growth is greater. Another reason for using the compound rather than the simple rate of growth is that the former can be discussed meaningfully alongside the yield, and allows a simple calculation of the total rate of return. This would not be the case with the simple rate of growth.

The pattern of performance of the share price can be determined by measuring the *real growth* rate from a range of dates to the end of the review period. The end of the review period is normally the latest date in the last quarter on which share prices were recorded, which, in the case of the *selected portfolio*, is 30 December 1992 in the printed Tables 13.2, 13.3 and 13.4, and 31 December 1993 in the tables on the floppy disk. Growth rates could, for instance, be calculated at intervals increasing by one year or for periods of one, three, six and nine years, all finishing on the same date. The *target growth* rate is also measured over the same intervals, so that the assessment of the performance of the share relative to the All Share Index is made easy.

THE CALCULATION OF THE REAL RETURN

The method used for calculating the *real return*, based on the addition of the *real growth* and the net yield, was outlined in Chapter 5. The theoretical basis for this method is developed in this section.

The return on an investment is defined as:

$$\text{Return} = \text{Pr}(y) - \text{Pr}(x) + D$$

where D is the net dividend paid between date x and date y, there being a gap of one year between x and y. It is assumed that, on average, dividends are paid mid-way between date x and date y, when the retail price index is $\text{RPI}(m)$. The calculation of the return in real terms uses the same logic as that used to calculate the *%real growth* on the first page of this appendix:

$$\text{Real return} = \text{Pr}(y) \times \text{RPI}(x) / \text{RPI}(y) - \text{Pr}(x) + D \times \text{RPI}(x) / \text{RPI}(m)$$

The %Real return per annum(RRet) is the Real return divided by $\text{Pr}(x)$ and mutiplied by 100:

$$\text{RRet}/100 = \text{Pr}(y)/\text{Pr}(x) \times \text{RPI}(x) / \text{RPI}(y) - 1 + D / \text{Pr}(x) \times \text{RPI}(x) / \text{RPI}(m)$$

If Y is the % net yield, then:

$$Y = 100 \times D / \text{Pr}(y), \text{ i.e. } D = Y \times \text{Pr}(y) / 100$$

Hence:

$$\text{RRet}/100 = \text{Pr}(y)/\text{Pr}(x) \times \text{RPI}(x)/\text{RPI}(y) - 1 + Y/100 \times \text{Pr}(y)/\text{Pr}(x) \times \text{RPI}(x)/\text{RPI}(m)$$

i.e. $\text{RRet}/100 + 1 = (\text{Pr}(y)/\text{Pr}(x) \times \text{RPI}(x)/\text{RPI}(y)) \times (1 + Y/100 \times \text{RPI}(y)/\text{RPI}(m))$

[Equation 5]

Again referring to the first page of this appendix, it was shown that:

$$\%\,\text{real growth/a} = 100 \times (\text{Pr}(y)/\text{Pr}(x) \times \text{RPI}(x)/\text{RPI}(y) - 1)$$

Using the abbreviation RGr for %Real growth/a, this equation can be written:

$$\text{RGr}/100 + 1 = (\text{Pr}(y)/\text{Pr}(x) \times \text{RPI}(x)/\text{RPI}(y))$$

This relationship can now be used to simplify Equation 5:

$\text{RRet}/100 + 1 = (\text{RGr}/100 + 1) \times (1 + Y/100 \times \text{RPI}(y)/\text{RPI}(m))$
i.e.
$\text{RRet}/100 = \text{RGr}/100 \times (1 + Y/100 \times \text{RPI}(y)/\text{RPI}(m)) + Y/100 \times \text{RPI}(y)/\text{RPI}(m)$
i.e.
$\text{RRet} = \text{RGr} \times (1 + Y/100 \times \text{RPI}(y)/\text{RPI}(m)) + Y \times \text{RPI}(y)/\text{RPI}(m)$

[Equation 6]

Now the annual rate of inflation, Infl, is:

$$\text{Infl} = (\text{RPI}(y) - \text{RPI}(x)) \times 100/\text{RPI}(x)$$

Since RPI(m) is half-way between RPI(x) and RPI(y), the equation can be redefined as:

$$\text{Infl} = (\text{RPI}(y) - \text{RPI}(m)) \times 200/\text{RPI}(m)$$
$$= 200 \times \text{RPI}(y)/\text{RPI}(m) - 200$$

Hence:

$$\text{RPI}(y)/\text{RPI}(m) = \text{Infl}/200 + 1$$

Substituting for RPI(y)/RPI(m) in Equation 6:

$$\text{RRet} = \text{RGr} \times (1 + Y/100\,(\text{Infl}/200 + 1)) + Y \times (\text{Infl}/200 + 1)$$

[Equation 7]

This relationship between the Real return, the Real growth and the net yield is often simplified to:

$$\%\,\text{Real return/a} = \%\,\text{Real growth/a} + \%\,\text{Yield (net)}$$

The error introduced by adopting the simplified version of the equation is discussed in more detail in Appendix 4. Many private investors will find the simplified version sufficiently accurate for most purposes.

The calculations carried out so far in this section have made use of the commonly accepted definition of the yield of a share:

$$\%\,\text{Yield} = \text{Dividend over last 12 months / Share price at end of 12 months}$$

If the calculations are repeated, but with the yield redefined as:

$$\%\,\text{Yield} = \text{Dividend over last 12 months / Average share price over the 12 months}$$

the result is an equation which produces figures for the *%real return* which are closer to those produced by the simplified equation. To put it another way, the simplified equation produces more accurate results when the denominator in the yield equation is the average share price, rather than the year-end share price, as is normal. Nevertheless the normal definition of the yield will continue to be used for individual shares, in order to avoid confusion and because figures for the yield, with this definition, are the ones that are published in the papers, magazines, etc. In calculating the yield of a portfolio, however, the denominator in the equation will be the average portfolio value, rather than the year-end value. This will result in more accurate figures for the Real return, firstly for the reason just outlined, and secondly because it will reduce the potential distortions that can arise when major purchases or sales cause large variations in the portfolio value.

APPENDIX 3

Portfolio performance – derivation of equations

This appendix explains the way in which the portfolio growth rates are calculated, giving more detail than in Chapter 6. Inevitably there is some duplication.

The value of a portfolio on a particular day can be calculated simply by adding together the values of the shares held in each company on that day (units in unit trusts are included in the share classification).

The measurement of the performance of a portfolio of shares is similar in principle to that just described for individual shares, but is different in detail and more complicated. The difference is a result of the fact that cash, in the form of purchases and sales of shares, is being injected or removed from the portfolio at intervals. For this reason the compound rate of growth of a portfolio cannot be calculated from the start value, the end value and the number of years between the two, as is the case for an individual share. The modification necessary to calculate the growth rate of a portfolio is simple and easy to implement when any investment that takes place is at the end of the year, and the only growth rate required is that over the past year. Increased complexity comes when the calculation has to be capable of dealing with investments at any time of the year, and when the growth rate to the end of the review period is required. Examples follow which will help the reader to understand the principles behind the calculations.

This appendix deals with the calculation of the growth rate of portfolios and the conversion of the growth rate figures into real growth rates, and explains the calculation of the target growth rates.

PORTFOLIO GROWTH RATE

The growth rate that is calculated in the example which follows is for the simplest option, in which there has been a single investment at the year-end into the portfolio.

One investment at year-end, growth rate over past year

If the %Portfolio growth/annum (PortGr) is required over exactly one year and the investment takes place at the end of the year, a simple adjustment to the method used for individual shares is all that is required. This adjustment requires the Invested (Inv) figure for the year to be subtracted from the year-end Portfolio value (Port), before the normal growth calculation is carried out. Hence, for the year beginning on date 'x' and ending on date 'x+1',

$$\%PortGr/a = (Port(x+10) - Port(x) - Inv) \times 100 / Port(x)$$
$$[\text{Equation 8}]$$

This equation allows the growth rate over one year to be calculated, uninfluenced by the investment that has taken place during the course of the year. (It should be noted that this is the growth rate and not the real growth rate.) An example of this type of calculation is shown in Table A3.1.

Table A3.1 Growth of portfolio over past year

Year End	1987	1988	1989	1990
Invested,£			300	
Port Value,£	1000	1100	1700	1500
Growth Rate over Past Year				
% Port growth/a.		10.0	27.3	−11.8

Definitions:
a) 'x' and 'x+1' are dates at the tops of columns, one year apart.
b) 'Invested,£' (Inv) is the net investment in the year ending in the date at the top of the column. Purchases are given a positive sign and sales a negative sign.
c) %Port growth/a=(Port(x+1)−Port(x)−Inv)×100/Port(x)

One investment at year-end, growth rate to end of review period

A better understanding of the performance of the portfolio is obtained by calculating the annual growth rates over various periods to the end-date, in addition to the growth rates over the past year shown in Table A3.1. In order to calculate the annual rate of growth between the date at the top of the column and the end-date (end-1990 in the case of the example in Table A3.1), it is necessary to assume a %Growth and calculate the value of the portfolio in successive years, the net investment being added at each appropriate year-end. The portfolio value, calculated in this way, at the end of the review period is then compared with the actual value of the portfolio and a succession of different %Growths are assumed until one is found which results in the two values being equal. This is known as a trial and error method. A growth rate measured in this way is the same in each of the years or part years in the review period. The figure for growth rate calculated by this method is a compound rate and is not distorted by investments within the period of the review.

   The growth rate calculations, which take little time on a computer, are described below. The first step is to carry out a quick exercise in mental arithmatic, which will give the order of magnitude of the %Growth/a. For instance:

Start Value	Investment	End Value
1987	1989	1990
£1000	£300	£1500

$$\text{Estimated Growth} = (1500 - 1000 - 300) \times 100 / 1000$$
$$= 20\,\%$$
$$\text{Estimated Growth /a.} = 20/3 = 6.7\,\% \text{ per annum}$$

This is not an accurate estimation of the growth rate because it ignores the compounding effect of the growth and also because the result is not influenced, as it should be, by the year in which the investment took place. It does, however, give a rate of growth figure (Gr), 6.7 per cent per annum, which can be used to start the trial and error method which leads to an accurate assessment of the growth rate. A very simple application of this method is now shown in Table

A3.2. It makes use of the same relationship defined in Equation 8 , which was used in the calculations in Table A3.1, but expressed in a different way, i.e.

$$\text{Port}(x+1) = \text{Port}(x) \times (1+\text{Gr}/100) + \text{Inv}$$
$$\text{where Gr} = \%\text{PortGrowth per annum} \qquad [\text{Equation 9}]$$

Table A3.2 Growth of portfolio to end of review period

Year End	1987	1988	1989	1990	Trial %growth/a
Investment,£			300		
Port value,£	1000	1100	1700	1500	
1stTrialValue,£	1000	1067	1438	1535	**6.7**
2ndTrialValue,£	1000	1060	1424	1509	**6.0**
3rdTrialValue,£	1000	1058	1419	1502	**5.8**

Definitions:
a) See Table A3.1 Definitions.
b) $\text{TrVal}(x+1) = \text{TrVal}(x) \times (1.0 + \text{Gr}/100) + \text{Investment}(x+1)$

The trial growth rate (Gr) is applied to the trial value at the end of each year to determine the trial value at the end of the following year, adding the Investment where appropriate. Different figures for the Trial %growth/a are tried. After a number of attempts the correct figure will be found, this being the one which results in the Trial Value at the end of the review period being equal to the Port value.

For the example in Table A3.2, taking the first trial growth rate at 6.7 per cent:

$$\text{TrVal}(1988) = 1000 \times (1.0 + 6.7/100) = £1067$$
$$\text{TrVal}(1989) = 1067 \times (1.0 + 6.7/100) + 300$$
$$= £1438$$
$$\text{TrVal}(1990) = 1438 \times (1.0 + 6.7/100) = £1535$$

This first trial gives a final Trial Value of £1535 which is £35 too high. The correct growth rate must therefore be below 6.7 per cent. The next trial, using a growth rate of 6 per cent per annum, produces a final Trial Value of £1,509, which is £9 too high. The correct growth rate, to one decimal place, is arrived at, in this case, on the third trial; the Trial Value is (within £2) equal to the portfolio value at the end of the review period, when the Growth is 5.8 per cent per annum over the three years.

This series of calculations can be carried out very quickly with a computer, by entering the location of the cell which contains the Trial %growth figure in the equations, rather than the figure itself. When a new figure is entered in this cell, the calculations will take place automatically; it is sometimes necessary to press the recalculation key on the computer.

Most investors will find that a quarterly frequency for producing this data is sufficient, whilst some will settle for an annual frequency, so that the trial and error calculations are not a great burden.

It is of interest to know how the growth has changed during the course of the review period. This data can be obtained by calculating the growth rate over the last two years and one year, as well as over the full review period of three years, as was done in the above calculations. The calculations of the intermediate growth rates are shown in the example in Table A3.3. In this case only the final trial figures are reproduced in the table.

Table A3.3 Intermediate portfolio growth rates

Year End	1987	1988	1989	1990	Trial %growths
Investment,£			300		
Port value,£	1000	1100	1700	1500	
Trial val,£					
Over 3 years	1000	1058	1419	1502	5.8
Over 2 years		1100	1443	1499	3.9
Over 1 year			1700	1499	−11.8

Definitions:

a) See Table A3.2 definitions.

b) The starting date is determined by the period over which the growth is being measured; i.e. over three years it is 1987, over two years 1988 and over one year 1989. When measuring the growth over two years, for instance, the start trial val of £1,100 is entered, equal to the portfolio value at the end of 1988.

In the example in Table A3.3, following the calculation of the growth rate over the full review period, the growth rate over two years is measured, using the second trial row. After entering £1,100 as the starting portfolio value, the growth rate over two years is determined by trial and error as 3.9 per cent per annum. Entering a starting value of £1,700 then allows the growth rate over the last year to be determined as −11.8 per cent per annum.

Presenting the tables of data in future, only two rows will be used for the trial values; this is explained in detail in Chapter 6.

One investment, any date, growth rate over past year

An investment that takes place during the course of a year would be expected to change in value during the remainder of the year, so that the equation used to calculate the growth rate must take this into account. Equation 8, used in the calculations in Table A3.1 for the portfolio growth rate (Gr) over the past year, when the investment (Inv) was made at the end of the year, was as follows:

$$\% \text{PortGr/a} = (\text{Port}(x+1) - \text{Port}(x) - \text{Inv}) \times 100 \,/\, \text{Port}(x)$$

The same relationship can be expressed in the following way:

$$\text{Port}(x+1) = \text{Port}(x) \times (1+\text{Gr}/100) + \text{Inv}$$

When the investment takes place D days before the end of the year, the investment grows at the same rate as the original portfolio, but only for a fraction D/365 of the year, and the equation becomes:

$$\text{Port}(x+1) = \text{Port}(x) \times (1+\text{Gr}/100) + \text{Inv}(1+\text{Gr}/100 \times D/365)$$

Hence:

$$
\begin{aligned}
\text{Port}(x+1) - \text{Port}(x) - \text{Inv} &= \text{Port}(x) \times \text{Gr}/100 + \text{Inv} \times \text{Gr}/100 \times D/365 \\
&= \text{Gr}/100 \times (\text{Port}(x) + \text{Inv} \times D/365) \\
&= \text{Gr}/100 \times (\text{Port}(x) + \text{InvFrac})
\end{aligned}
$$

where InvFrac (Investment Fraction),£ = Investment × D/365

Hence:

$$\% \text{Growth/a} = 100 \times (\text{Port}(x+1) - \text{Port}(x) - \text{Inv}) / (\text{Port}(x) + \text{InvFrac})$$
[Equation 10]

The same equation can be used for purchases or sales, the latter being treated as negative investments. In the example in Table A3.4, suppose the portfolio values and the amount of the investment are the same as in Table A3.3, but the investment was made 250 days before the end of the year.

Table A3.4 Investment in portfolio partway through year

Year End	1987	1988	1989	1990
Invested,£			300	
InvFract,£			205	
Port value,£	1000	1100	1700	1500
Growth Rate over past year				
% Port growth/a		10.0	23.0	−11.8

Definitions:
a) See definitions appended to Table A3.1.
b) % Growth/a = 100×(Port(x+1)−Port(x)−Inv) / (Port(x) + InvFrac)

The effect of investing the £300 part-way through the year, instead of at the end of the year, reduces the growth rate in the year ending 1989 from 27.3 to 23.0 per cent (comparing Table A3.4 with Table A3.1). As would be expected, the growth rates in 1988 and 1990 are unaltered.

One investment, any date, growth rate to end of review period

The calculations in Table A3.5 are carried out with the same portfolio values and investment profile as that used in the example in Table A3.4, but in this case the calculations lead to the annual growth rate over a range of years, all finishing on the date the review period ends. As explained earlier the trial and error method of calculation is required. Table A3.5 is the same as Table 6.3, but is reproduced here

to aid the continuity of the explanations. The calculations leading to
the growth rates are explained in detail immediately after Table 6.3.

Table A3.5 Investment in portfolio partway through year, growth to end of review period

Year end	1987	1988	1989	1990	Trial %growths
Investment,£			300		
Inv Frac.,£			205		
Port value,£	1000	1100	1700	1500	
Trial val,£					
Over 3 years	1000	1054	1422	1499	**5.4**
Over 2 years		1100	1447	1499	**3.6**
Over 1 year			1700	1499	**−11.8**

Definitions:
a) See Table A3.3 definitions.
b) The following equation is used in the trial and error calculations:
   $\text{Port}(x+1) = \text{Port}(x) + \text{Inv} + \text{Gr}/100 \times (\text{Port}(x) + \text{InvFrac}(x))$

Comparing the results in Table A3.3 with those in Table A3.5, it is
seen that the effect of investing part-way through the year, rather
than at the end of the year, is to reduce the growth rates over three
and two years by 0.4 and 0.3 respectively. As would be expected,
there is no difference in the growth rate over one year.

Table A3.6 Investment data from MspData file

	Investment date	Inv,£ (1988)	InvFrac,£ (1988)
Share A	02/05/88	100	67
Share B	19/08/88	200	73
Share C	13/10/88	−250	−54
Share D	15/02/88	150	132
Total		200	217

Definitions:
a) Inv,£ details all the investments that took place during 1988. Purchases are
   positive and sales negative.
b) The figures for the total investment and investment fraction for each year are
   transferred to the *MspPort* file, where the growth figures are calculated.

Some of the data needed to carry out the calculations leading to the *selected portfolio* growths is collected in the *MspData* file (Table 13.2), in the form shown in the example in Table A3.6.

REAL GROWTH AND TARGET GROWTH RATES

Having calculated the trend in the growth rate of the portfolio, the real growth rate can now be calculated. The target growth rate of the portfolio is also calculated, to provide a basis for comparison.

The way in which the real growth rate of a share price is calculated from the growth rate of the share price and the rate of inflation has been explained in Chapter 5 and Appendix 2. When calculating the *real growth* of a portfolio over the past year, the same equations as were used for a share are valid, the portfolio growth rate being substituted in the equation for the share growth rate.

The calculation of the real portfolio growth rate over the period to the end of the review period is also carried out using the same equations as were used for the individual share. This is valid because the method of calculation is such that the portfolio growth rate in any one year is the same as in any other year or over the whole review period, providing these years are between the starting date and the end date of the review period. This observation follows directly from the way in which the growth rate is calculated. The calculations that were derived for a single share, therefore, relating the *real growth* to the growth of the share price and to inflation, (Equation 3, Appendix 2), apply equally well to the calculation of the *real growth* of a portfolio, whether the review period is the past year or a number of years. The relationship for an individual share was recorded in the Definitions appended to Table 5.5. Substituting the portfolio growth rate in the equation for the share price growth rate gives:

$$\% \text{Real portGr/a} = 100 \times (\text{PortGr} - \text{Infl}) / (100 + \text{Infl})$$

The *target growth* is the figure that the *real growth* would have achieved if the prices of the shares in the portfolio had moved in line with, or tracked, the All Share Index. For the reasons outlined above, the calculations that were derived for a single share, relating the *target growth* to the growth rate of the All Share Index and to inflation, apply equally well to the calculation of the *target growth* of a portfolio. The *target growth* can be calculated, therefore, by substituting in the above equation the AlShI growth for the portfolio growth rate:

$$\% \text{Targ Growth/a} = 100 \times (\text{AlShIGr} - \text{Infl}) / (100 + \text{Infl})$$

As expected, this equation is identical to that used for individual shares, (Equation 4, Appendix 2).

The calculations of the *real growth* and *target growth*, for the same portfolio as used in the example in Table A3.5, are shown in Table A3.7.

Table A3.7 Real and target growths of portfolios

Year end	1987	1988	1989	1990
Investment,£			300	
RPI	103.3	110.6	119.1	130.1
AlShI	891	926	1205	1038
Port value,£	1000	1100	1700	1500
Trial val,£	1000	1000	1300	1300
Trial val,£			1700	1499
% Growth/a. to end-1990			Trial %	5.8
Port val	**5.8**	**3.9**	−11.8	
RPI (Infl)	8.0	8.5	9.2	
AlShI	5.2	5.9	−13.8	
Real	−2.0	−4.2	−19.3	
Target	−2.6	−2.4	−21.1	
Gross yield,%	4.5	4.8	4.6	4.9
Target yield,%	4.2	4.6	4.2	5.4

Definitions:

a) See definitions appended to Tables A3.3 and A3.4 for port growth calculations.

b) See Table 5.5 for definitions for RPI and AlShI rates of growth.

c) % Real growth $= 100 \times (\text{PortGr} - \text{Infl}) / (100 + \text{Infl})$

d) % Targ growth $= 100 \times (\text{AlShIGr} - \text{Infl}) / (100 + \text{Infl})$

The trial and error procedure allows the %Port growth/a, to be calculated over various periods, which start on a range of dates but which all end on the same date at the end of the review period. In practice, all the calculations leading to the %Port growth rates can be accomplished by allocating only two rows to the TrialVal figures, as shown in Table A3.7. This results in a significant saving in space when analysing data which covers a few years, as is the case for the *selected portfolio*, for instance. The first row records the figures derived by applying the formulae already outlined, to calculate the portfolio growth rate over the full period of the review. The figures in this row only change when a different Trial %growth is inserted in the cell allocated for this purpose (the cell in the last column in Table A3.7, containing the figure 5.8).

The second row is used to calculate the %Port growth over the shorter periods. It contains the same set of calculations as the first row initially. To calculate the %Port growth/a over two years, for instance, the value of the portfolio at the end of 1988 of £1100 is inserted in the second trial row and the trial and error method applied to determine the %Port growth/a from the end of 1988 to the end of 1990. The answer is 3.9 per cent. The same procedure is followed to determine the growth rate over one year (-11.8 per cent). The trial values for this calculation are shown in the second trial row in Table A3.7.

The procedures outlined in the previous paragraph have the effect of erasing the equations relating the values in the second trial row to each other, with the exception of the 1990 value. The original equations are, however, still in the computer's memory for the first trial row, so that they can be checked or modified at any time. If it is necessary to recalculate the intermediate growth rates, the second row equations can be copied from the first row.

Having calculated the %Port growth/a, the %inflation (% RPI growth/a) and the %AlShI growth/a are then calculated, which in turn allows the *real growth* and the *target growth* figures to be determined. A commentary on the performance of the portfolio, based on the criteria just explained and calculated in Table A3.7, can be found in Chapter 6.

The net yield of the portfolio, in any one year, is calculated by adding together the dividends paid on each of the share holdings and then dividing by the value of all the shares in the portfolio. For comparison the *target yield* (net) is also recorded. The gross yield can be calculated, if required, by adding back the tax credits and then continuing the calculation in the same way. The calculation for the *selected portfolio* (Table 13.4) uses the dividends in the tax year and the value at the end of the calendar year. The tax year dividends were calculated because they were needed for the tax return. A more rigorous treatment would use either the dividends in the calendar year together with the average portfolio value in the calendar year, or the dividends in the tax year together with the average portfolio value in the tax year. Adoption of the more rigorous approach would result in only a small improvement in accuracy, in the case of the *selected portfolio*.

As mentioned at the beginning of this Appendix, there has been some duplication with the contents of Chapter 6. This is because both the Appendix and the Chapter cover the same subject, but the Appendix has given a more detailed explanation of the way in which the equations have been derived.

CALCULATING THE REAL RETURN USING THE IRR METHOD

The direct method recommended for measuring the *real growth* of a portfolio was outlined in Chapter 6, whilst the principles on which the method is based have just been discussed. That method is called the T&E method, T&E being short for 'trial and error'. The method uses a trial and error calculation and can accommodate major investments at irregular intervals.

The direct method for measuring the *real return* of a portfolio is the IRR method. IRR is the name of the function in the Lotus spreadsheet for calculating the internal rate of return of a range of cash flows. The fact that there is a function for this calculation in many computer programmes available to private investors, means that the calculations can be carried out quite quickly compared to the T&E method. The IRR method can only deal with cash flows at regular intervals, however, which means that the calculated rates of return are not very accurate unless:

a) Small intervals are used, e.g. a quarter, or still better, a month. This is a disadvantage in that it can increase the data that requires to be entered and kept in the computer memory.

b) Less frequent intervals, even annual, can be used if the values of any purchases or sales are small compared with the value of the portfolio. This limitation is less important when the cash from a sale is immediately reinvested in different shares which are included in the same portfolio.

Most private investors will find that the IRR method of calculation is of sufficient accuracy, providing the intervals are quarterly or less.

Readers are reminded that the direct method of calculation only has to be used for one of the two principal performance criteria, *real growth* or *real return*. For instance, once the *real growth* has been calculated by the direct method, the *real return* can be derived from the *real growth* and the yield, rather than by the direct method.

Some simple examples of using the IRR function are shown in Table A3.8. The cash flow at the beginning of the review period is the value of the portfolio (as if it had been purchased), and is negative. The net-of-tax dividends are positive cash flows whilst the net (i.e. purchases minus sales) investments are negative cash flows. The cash flow for the last period of the review is equal to the value of the portfolio (as if it had been sold), plus the net dividends and minus the net investment in the last period.

In Table A3.9 the IRR method is used to calculate the *real return* of the *selected portfolio*, over the last four years of the review period.

Table A3.8 Examples of the rate of return (IRR) calculation

	Cash flow					Return/a
	£	£	£	£	£	%
	End '85	End '86	End '87	End '88	End '89	Over 4 Years
No dividends or investment						
Capital	−1000	0	0	0	1464	
Cash flow	−1000	0	0	0	1464	**10.0**
With dividends						
Capital	−1000	0	0	0	1464	
Net divi	0	100	110	121	133	
Cash flow	−1000	100	110	121	1597	**20.0**
With investment						
Capital	−1000	−1000	0	0	2795	
Net divi	0	0	0	0	0	
Cash flow	−1000	−1000	0	0	2795	**10.0**
With dividends and investment						
Capital	−1000	−1000	0	0	2795	
Net divi	0	100	210	231	254	
Cash flow	−1000	−900	210	231	3049	**20.0**

Definitions and assumptions:

a) Investments are made at the year-end, before the portfolio is valued.

b) Dividends are paid at the year-end.

c) The rate of return is calculated using the Lotus 'Internal Rate of Return', i.e. the IRR, function. For instance, for the range of values of cash flow shown in the last line of the Table:

$$\% \text{ Return/a.} = @IRR(\text{Guess Return, Range}) = 20 \text{ per cent}$$

where the range is the range of figures starting with − 1000 and finishing with 3,049.

The calculation of the *%target return*, is identical to that described in Chapter 5 for use in the assessment of the performance of individual shares.

Table A3.9 The real return (IRR) of the selected portfolio

	30/12/88	29/12/89	28/12/90	27/12/91	30/12/92
Port value,£	51439	64117	53828	58753	71978
Past year					
Invested,£	329	208	687	721	625
Net divi,£	1779	2212	2394	2451	2377
Period to 30/12/92					
Years	4.0	3.0	2.0	1.0	
Cash flow,£	− 51439	2004	1706	1730	73730
		−64117	1706	1730	73730
			−53828	1730	73730
				−58753	73730
%Return/a	11.9	6.5	18.7	25.5	
%Real return/a	5.8	1.3	15.0	22.9	
%Targ return/a	7.4	2.5	14.4	18.3	
%Infl/a	5.8	5.2	3.2	2.1	
%AlShI growth/a	10.0	4.1	14.3	17.2	
%AlShI return/a	13.6	7.7	18.1	20.8	
RPI	110.6	119.1	130.1	135.7	138.6
AlShI	926	1205	1038	1157	1358
% Yield(net)					
Portfolio	3.5	3.5	4.4	4.2	3.3
Target	3.5	3.2	4.1	3.9	3.3

Definitions and assumptions:

a) The figures for the portfolio value, invested, net dividend, RPI, AlShI, infl(ation), %net yield (portfolio) and %net yield (target) are all transposed from Table 13.4.

b) The Cash flow on the first date of the review period is equal to the portfolio value on that date. For instance, when measuring the %Return between 28/12/90 and 30/12/92, the first figure in the range of cash flows is the portfolio value on 28/12/90, i.e. −£53,828.
The second figure in the range of cash flows is:

$$= \text{Net Divi} - \text{Invested} = 2451 - 721 = 1730$$

The third figure in the range of cash flows is:

$$= \text{Portfolio value} + \text{Net divi} - \text{invested}$$
$$= 71978 + 2377 - 625 = 73730$$

The Lotus function is then:

$$\% \text{ Return/a} = @ \text{ IRR (Guess rate, Range)}$$
$$= @ \text{ IRR (20 \%, } -53828 .. 73730)$$
$$= 18.7 \%$$

c) The *real return* can now be calculated, using the same equation as described in Chapter 5 and as derived from first principles in Appendix 2; i.e.

%real return = (Return − Infl) / (1 + Infl / 100)

d) The target figures are calculated as follows:

Firstly use the @ Rate function to calculate the rate of growth of the AlShI. Then calculate the %return of the AlShI:

% AlShI return/a = AlShI growth/a + average targ yield (net)

The %target return can now be calculated:

%targ return = (AlShI return − Infl) / (1 + Infl / 100)

The accuracy of the calculation of the real return

EQUITY INVESTMENTS

When measuring the performance of individual shares, the *real return* has been defined as the addition of the *real growth* and the net yield, the latter figure being taken as the average of the net yields during the period over which the *real return* is being measured. This method of calculation of the *real return* is an approximation and is adopted because the calculation is simpler and more easily carried out than the mathematically correct method, which is complicated by each share having different dividend payment dates. This Appendix is included to give readers an indication of the error involved in the calculation of the *real return*, and also to outline a method that can be used to determine the degree of error in any particular set of circumstances.

The approximate relationship is:

$$\%\text{real return/a} = \%\text{real growth/a} + \%\text{yield (net)}$$

The valid relationship between these variables was calculated in Appendix 2, (see Equation 7), and was as follows:

$$\text{RRet} = \text{RGr} \times (1 + Y/100\,(\text{Infl}/200 + 1)) + Y \times (\text{Infl}/200 + 1)$$

where RRet = %real return/a, RGr = %real growth/a, Y = %yield (net) and Infl = %inflation/a.

An indication of the errors that can arise, as a result of using the approximate relationship, is shown in the examples in Table A4.1. The examples in Table A4.1 permutate the three variables Real growth, Yield and Inflation. In both Examples 1 and 2, for instance, the *real growth* is assumed to be 4 per cent per annum and the yield

Table A4.1 The errors in the real return calculations

Examples	1	2	3	4	5
% Real growth/a	4	4	8	8	8
% Yield (net)	6	6	2	2	6
% Inflation/a	2	10	2	10	10
(Infl/200 + 1)	1.01	1.05	1.01	1.05	1.05
Y × (Infl/200 + 1)	6.06	6.30	2.02	2.10	6.30
%real return/a	**10.30**	**10.55**	**10.18**	**10.27**	**14.80**

(net) 6 per cent per annum. In Example 1, however, the Inflation is assumed to be 2 per cent per annum, whereas in Example 2 it is assumed to be 10 per cent per annum.

A quick mental calculation shows that the approximate relationship produces figures for the *real return* of 10 per cent per annum for Examples 1 to 4 and 14 per cent for Example 5. In Chapter 6 the real return calculated in this way is termed the %real return (T&E). The figures in the line '%real return/a' are obtained using the accurate equation (see above). The errors resulting from the use of the approximate equation:

$$\% \text{ Real return/a} = \% \text{ Real growth/a} + \% \text{ Yield (net)}$$

are seen to range from 1.8 per cent to 5.5 per cent for Examples 1 to 4. The simplified equation produces a Real return of 14 per cent per annum for Example 5, so that the error is 5.7 per cent. The use of the approximate equation is seen to result in the real return being underestimated. Investors looking for a higher standard of accuracy have the option of using the accurate equation shown above.

An alternative, not considered so far in this section, is to use the Lotus function @IRR to measure the *real return* of an individual share (see Chapter 6). In order to obtain a higher degree of accuracy than that achieved with the simplified equation quoted above, it would be necessary to record dividends monthly. It was decided that this would be an unecessary complication for the majority of investors, the benefit being only a small increase in accuracy, and this option was not therefore pursued.

The use of the IRR method for measuring the *real return* of portfolios was described in detail in Chapter 6. The accuracy of the method can be improved if small intervals are used, e.g. a quarter or better still, a month. This can be a disadvantage for some investors, in that it can increase the data that requires to be entered and kept in the computer memory. Quarterly intervals are quite sufficient if the values of any purchases or sales are small compared with the value of the portfolio. This limitation is less important when the cash from a sale is immediately reinvested in different shares which are included in the same portfolio. It was decided that the IRR calculation should be carried out quarterly instead of annually. The only extra information needed is the recording of the dividends paid per quarter. Due to the compounding effect a *real return* of 2 per cent per quarter, for example, is equivalent to an annual rate of 8.24 per cent. It is suggested that an investor should never use less than a quarterly frequency with the IRR method, partly in the interest of accuracy, but also because it gives a better picture of the trend of the *real return* with time. A compromise is, however available, i.e. a quarterly frequency could be used for the last, say, two or three years with an annual frequency prior to that. There would be a significant gain in accuracy compared with the use of an annual frequency throughout.

The IRR method is essentially the 'discounted cash flow' (DCF) method of analysis. This was developed to allow different business investment proposals to be compared and is described in detail in many books on financial management, accounting, capital investment appraisal, etc. (e.g *Capital Budgeting and Company Finance*, by A.J. Merrett and Allen Sykes, (Longman, 1966). The DCF return on a project is defined as the annual return on the capital outstanding at the end of each year of the project's life.

The IRR function could be used to measure the growth rate in the value of the portfolio, instead of the T&E method. The investments would have to be allocated to equal time intervals, such as quarters, as was done when measuring the rate of return by the IRR method. Dividends would not be included in the calculation. This alternative would have the advantage that the Lotus function 'IRR' would require less time and effort by the investor than the T&E calculation. The disadvantage is that the accuracy would be less, unless short time intervals were used. The T&E method has been adopted for inclusion in the System because the private investor's portfolio is quite likely to be subject on occasions to large inflows and outflows of cash. Examples of the causes of such large changes in the portfolio are investments of money from legacies, retirement and golden hand-shakes, and sales resulting from house purchase, job loss and planning to reduce inheritance tax. These are the very conditions that can lead to large errors as a result of using the 'IRR' function to calculate the growth rate.

Another alternative considered was to use the T&E method to measure the rate of return of the portfolio directly, rather than by making use of the equation relating the % return to the sum of the % growth and the net yield. The time and effort required by the investor to deal with the dividends in the same way as the investments ruled out this option. Furthermore, the dividends will normally be much more evenly spread than the investments, so that they can be allocated to time intervals of quarters, or even years, without a serious loss of accuracy when using the IRR method for calculating the rate of return.

FIXED INTEREST INVESTMENTS

This section of the book is concerned with the application, to fixed interest investments, of the methods of performance assessment that have been developed for equities. The results are compared with those obtained using more conventional methods of performance assessment. The calculations in the example in Table A4.2 are carried out using a mathematically correct method, whilst those in Table A4.3 use the approximate relationship of the *real return* to the *real growth* and the Yield. The criterion calculated in this way is called the *real return* (T&E) and the definition follows the first paragraph of this Appendix. Both tables calculate the performance of a bank account in which the net interest is retained. For bank or building society savings accounts, the %net interest rate is substituted for the %net yield, these two variables being equal in this particular type of investment. The interest rate is assumed to be the three-month inter-bank rate. In Table A4.2 the performance is expressed in terms of the growth in the real value of the account, whilst in Table A4.3 it is expressed in terms of the *real return* (T&E). The performance figures expressed in these two ways should produce identical results, since the net interest is retained in the account.

In Table A4.2 the balance in the bank account is calculated on each review date, after adding the annual interest. Scaling these figures to the RPI allows the balance in the bank account to be expressed in terms of the real value of the £ on 30 December 1988. The Growth/a in the real value of the bank account is then calculated, over the period from the date at the top of the column to the end date, i.e. 30 December 1992.

Table A4.2 Growth in real value of £100 in bank account

	30/12/88	29/12/89	28/12/90	27/12/91	30/12/92
Years to 30/12/92	4.0	3.0	2.0	1.0	
% Interest,gross	13.0	15.1	14.0	10.9	7.1
Value of account	100.0	110.5	122.6	134.0	143.1
RPI	110.6	119.1	130.1	135.7	138.6
Real val of Acc't.	100.0	102.6	104.2	109.3	114.2
%Growth/a. in Real value over period to 30/12/92					
	3.4	3.6	4.6	4.5	

Definitions:

a) Basic rate income tax = 25 %.

b) The gross interest rates are the three month inter-bank rates. The rate of interest over a year is taken as the average of the rate at the beginning and end of the year. The net interest is retained in the account.

c) Real value(x) = Value(x) × RPI(30/12/88) / RPI(x)

d) Over the years to the end review date:
$\quad$ %Gr.in real val = @Rate(Real val(30/12/92),Real val(x),Years)×100
where x is the date at the top of the column.

In Table A4.3 it is first of all assumed that the dividend is distributed; consequently there is zero growth in the bank balance. The real growth of the bank balance can then be calculated from a knowledge of the rate of inflation, this of course being negative. The *%real return* is then calculated from the %real growth and the %net yield.

Table A4.3 Real return on bank savings accounts

	30/12/88	29/12/89	28/12/90	27/12/91	30/12/92
Years to 30/12/92	4.0	3.0	2.0	1.0	
% Interest,gross	13.0	15.1	14.0	10.9	7.1
RPI	110.6	119.1	130.1	135.7	138.6
Over period to 30/12/92					
% Infl/a	5.8	5.2	3.2	2.1	
Avg.%Interest	12.5	12.0	10.7	9.0	
% Real growth/a	−5.5	−4.9	−3.1	−2.1	
% Real return/a	**3.9**	**4.1**	**4.9**	**4.7**	

Definitions:

a) Basic rate income tax = 25 %.

b) %Real growth/a = (Growth/a − Infl) / (1 + Infl/100)
    The Growth/a is zero for a bank account.

c) %Real ret = %Real growth/a + % Net yield (average).

d) The net yield is the net rate of interest.

The % Growth in *real value* calculated in Table A4.2 should be equal to the %Real return calculated in Table A4.3. Comparing the figures it is seen that the two methods of calculation produce differences ranging from 0.2 to 0.5 percentage points. Only one quarter of the difference is accounted for by the use of the simplified equation (definition c). The error is not large but this was one of the reasons for deciding to express Real returns in integers, i.e. to nil decimal places. The method of calculation of the Real return shown in Table A4.3, was chosen for the System because it simplifies the calculations. The alternative of using the method shown in Table A4.2 might not seem very complicated in this example, but in practice would be difficult, due particularly to the problem of dealing with two dividend payments per share, paid on a wide variety of dates. Further complications arise when the shares or stocks are traded on the stock exchange at prices which vary from day to day, in contrast to the bank savings accounts shown in Tables A4.2 and A4.3.

The assumption made in the calculations that the dividends are all received on a single day each year is a source of error which affects both methods. This results, on average, in an underestimate of the *%real return/a* of about 0.2 percentage points; i.e. a *real return* shown by the calculations to be 10 per cent per annum should on average, be about 10.2 per cent.

This section makes no claim to be a rigorous analysis of the potential inaccuracies of the method of calculation of the *real return*. Readers can, however, use this same approach to determine whether the accuracy is sufficient for any particular set of circumstances they might meet.

The potential errors that have been outlined in this section of the book are, of course, all a consequence of the assumptions which were made in the calculations, with the objective of ensuring that they do not become too time-consuming or complicated for the private investor. Every effort has been made to strike the right balance for the private investor, between the need to achieve satisfactory accuracy whilst avoiding too much complication in the calculations.

APPENDIX 5

Alternative methods for monitoring share performance

P/A RATIO – REBASING

Chapter 5 describes how the P/A ratio is used to monitor the perform-ance of individual shares. The 'Price(c)/AlShI' ratios are rebased to 1.0 at the end of 1990 in the calculation of the P/A ratio for the System. There are two obvious alternative dates that were considered but rejected. These are the start of the review period or the end. Each alternative has its advantages and disadvantages. Rebasing to 1.00 at the end allows shares purchased after the start of the review period to be easily included in the comparison since such shares, after being rebased, will have a ratio of 1.00 at the end of the review period, as do the other shares. Rebasing to 1.00 at the end has the disadvantage, however, that there is an increase in workload because the computer must be reprogrammed to calculate the ratios each time the latest share prices are entered, although the computer copying facility means that this would not add greatly to the work load. When the rebasing takes place from the start it is easier to interpret the results, since an increase in the ratio from, say, 1.00 to 1.17 can be described as an increase in the price of the shares, relative to the index, of 17 per cent. With rebasing at the end of the review period the change in ratio would have been from 0.86 to 1.0, making the discussion of perform-ance somewhat more difficult. Rebasing to 1.00 at the start of the review period is not possible for shares purchased after this date, but this disadvantage can be overcome by rebasing such shares to the average of the other shares on the first data entry date after the date of purchase; this does, however, introduce complexity at the cost of easy understanding.

It was decided that the balance of advantage lay with a compromise, in which re-basing to 1.00 takes place at a notable date, e.g. the end of the calendar or tax year, two or three years before the end of the review period. The work involved in changing the date of the rebasing would then only be required once every two years. This decision has the following advantages:

a) If rebasing to 1.00 took place on 31 March 1982, for instance, some shares would have *P/A ratios* of, say, 0.3 by 1991, whilst others would have a ratio of, say, 2.5. A fall in ratio of 0.1 would then have a very different significance in these two cases. In view of the fact that one of the most important uses of the P/A ratio is to monitor recent changes in the share price on a short-term basis, it is considered that this should be made as easy as possible and adopting the proposal to re-base at a recent notable date will achieve this.

b) One of the minor objectives of the System is to avoid modifying data, for convenience, in a way which could cause confusion and misunderstanding. Rebasing newly purchased shares to the average of all the shares in the category would breach this objective, and would not be necessary if the recommended System of rebasing at the latest notable date is adopted.

EFFECT OF RIGHTS ISSUES ON CORRECTED PRICE

When a company makes a rights issue it can affect the *corrected price* of the shares. For instance, if a share is trading at 400p before the rights issue and one new share is offered at 300p for every four shares already held, then the ex-rights share price will be:

$$= ((4 \times 400) + (1 \times 300)) / 5 = 1900 / 5 = 380p$$

Each investor can decide whether the effect of the rights issue on the corrected share price is large enough to make it worthwhile to make the appropriate adjustments. In the *MspPri* file (Table 13.3 for the *selected portfolio*) there is a standard approach to the issuing of scrip shares. The effect of the rights issue just mentioned is equivalent to a scrip issue of one share for every x shares held, where:

$$x = \text{corrected price} / (\text{price} - \text{corrected price})$$
$$= 380 / (400 - 380) = 19$$

In other words, the rights issue can be treated in the *MspPri* file, as if it were a scrip issue of one share for every 19 held already.

USE OF 'PRICE/RPI' RATIO FOR SHARES

The method of analysis outlined in Chapter 5 makes use of the *P/A ratio* as one of the criteria for reviewing the performance of individual shares. This method is easy to use and to understand and is useful when investors want to monitor their shares from week to week, or even from day to day, with a view to deciding the optimum time to buy or sell a particular holding. It is primarily for this reason that it was selected for inclusion in the System.

Having decided to include the *P/A ratio* in the System, it was obvious that the use of the ratio 'Price/RPI' should also be con-sidered, to give an indication of how the real value of the shares has changed over a period of time. This is demonstrated in Table A5.1, the prices and dates being the same as those used in Table 5.2.

Table A5.1   Ratio of share price to RPI

	Year End		1991		
	1989	1990	22/11	29/11	6/12
Price(c)	750	800	900	850	800
AlShI	1205	1038	1183	1169	1149
RPI	119.1	130.1	135.9	136.0	136.1
P/A ratio	0.81	1.00	0.99	0.94	0.90
Pr(c)/RPI (re-based)	1.02	1.00	1.08	1.02	0.96
%Net yield		2.9	2.7	2.9	3.0

The *P/A ratio* shows that the shares performed better than the All Share Index by about 11 per cent (0.81 rising to 0.90), over the period of the review. The price peaked at the end of 1990, and since then the shares have lost 10 per cent of their value, relative to the All Share Index.

The Price(c)/RPI ratio shows the fall in the real value of the shares over the full period of the review, but a further calculation would be necessary to express this fall in generally understood terms. The *real growth* method of performance assessment does just this, and was therefore chosen for inclusion in the System, rather than the Price/RPI ratio.

CONVENTIONAL METHODS

General

The conventional method most frequently used for measuring the financial performance of an investment is to calculate the total return on the investment. This criterion is not included in the System, because the return after allowing for the effect of inflation has been preferred, i.e. the *real return*. There could, however, be investors who would prefer to use the conventional criteria, for a variety of reasons. For instance, they might have used the conventional method in their business and feel more comfortable with it, having established their own set of standards for comparison. Such investors will find the methods for calculating the conventional criteria in this book, because they are intermediate steps towards the calculation of the chosen criteria. The most important message in the book is that the measurement of performance is of great importance to success in investing. The choice of criteria is of secondary importance, and the return per annum is a valid alternative to the *real return per annum*. Those investors who choose to use the return/a as one of the principal criteria of performance can, of course, adopt the the %target return/a as a suitable standard, this being the %return/a achieved by a share which tracks the All Share Index. (This is different to the *target return*, as defined in this book, which is the *real return* of a share which tracks the All share Index. This would more correctly have been termed the *target real return*, but the briefer version was chosen to save space, particularly in the vertical headings of the tables).

Capital growth with reinvestment of dividends

One of the methods used to evaluate the performance of a company's shares is to calculate the value of a nominal holding of shares, over a period of time, on the assumption that the net dividends are reinvested in the purchase of more shares in the same company. This method is much used by the financial magazines for unit trusts and investment trusts, where the value of, say, £100 invested one month, three months, six months, one year, three years and seven years ago is shown in a table for a variety of trusts. For instance the values of an initial investment of £100, over periods of three and seven years to 1 January 1993, with net income reinvested, are shown below. The figures are abstracted from the *Money Observer* for February, 1993, to whom they were provided by PSDS.

Table A5.2 Value of £100 investment in unit trusts

Years to 1/1/93	3 Years		7 Years	
Unit Trust	£	Ranking	£	Ranking
HendInGr	107.3	504	219.9	187
InvGrBrC	111.7	408	212.8	220
SPInvTr	107.7	491	218.4	192
MGCompGr	105.2	548	201.0	281
MGRec'y	99.6	648	264.4	54
Number of funds		1133		657
Average	104.3		198.6	
Investment in AlShI	115.9		227.4	

There are a number of general objections to this method of performance appraisal:

a) The method gives no indication of the growth of the value of the investment in real terms.

b) The method does not include the comparison of the performance with readily available and easily understood standards, outside

the field of equity investments, as is the case when the performance of the shares and portfolios is expressed in terms of the *real
growth* or *real return*, as recommended by the System.

Two possible ways in which this method could be used will be considered: firstly the use of the magazine figures directly, and secondly
the calculation of the figures by investors specifically for the shares in
their portfolio.

With regard to the possibility of investors using the value after
reinvestment quoted in the magazines for their own shares, this is
very seldom a reliable indication of how the units have performed,
since the date on which the investor bought the units is very unlikely
to coincide with the date on which the investment was made in the
magazine's figures. This, of course, can have a major effect on the
performance figures. For instance, the magazine's figures might show
a growth in a unit's value of 30 per cent over a period of four years, as
calculated from 30 September 1987. However, if the investor's units
were in fact purchased two months later than the magazine's units, on
26 November 1987, the growth would have been nearer to 50 or 60
per cent. Investors will also often want to know how their shares have
performed up to a date of their own choosing, rather than have to
wait until a magazine has been published, and then find that the
figures in the magazine are weeks out-of-date. Another disadvantage
of this approach is the fact that the performance data in magazines is
normally confined to unit and investment trusts, figures for ordinary
shares not being available over the longer time periods. The
magazine's figures are, of course, completely unsuitable for the
assessment of the performance of portfolios. Use of the figures in a
magazine does have the merit, however, of assessing the relative
performances of a wide range of unit and investment trusts over an
extended period of time. This is particularly useful in assisting an
investor in choosing a trust to buy.

The second alternative, where the investor himself calculates the
values of the nominal holding, is not attractive for the following
reasons:

a)   The calculations are significantly more complicated than those required for implementing the System, especially for shares or stocks which have a variable price, e.g equities, gilts, and preference shares.

b) as already mentioned, the data obtained is in a less useful form than that derived by the System.

The conclusion is that investors are recommended to determine the performance of their own shares and portfolio, using the methods chosen for the System.

Investors who would like to use the 'Reinvestment of Dividends' method, however, can carry out the calculations themselves. This can be done by using a modified *MspPri* file. The design of the file and many of its calculations are the same as for normal use; it is named Measuring Share Performance; Share-Reinvestment i.e *'MspShReI'*. The differences between this file and *'MspPri'* are in the rules concerning the way in which the data is manipulated in the file. These are described in the following paragaphs.

All net dividends are reinvested. Any investments in new shares or sales of existing shares are ignored, other than the shares purchased by reinvesting the net dividend. The holding therefore comprises the original holding at the start of the review period, any scrip issue shares, and shares obtained by reinvesting the dividends.

The dividends reinvested are calculated from the dividend per share and the number of shares held, as defined in Definition (b) for Table A5.3. This calculation cannot necessarily be carried out from a knowledge of the cash dividends since the latter could include dividends received for shares purchased with 'new' money. An example of the calculation is shown in Table A5.3.

From Table 5.3 it is seen that the values for successive years, with the target values in brackets, are: £100(£100), £115.0 (£108.7), £142.6 (£147.4), and £136.9 (£133.2). Monitoring the performance of a share by calculating the value of the holding, after reinvestment of the dividends, and comparing these values with those that would have obtained if the shares had tracked the All Share Index is seen to be of limited benefit.

The calculation shown in the example in Table A5.3 is much less complicated than it would be in practice, because it has been assumed

Table A5.3 Value of £100 with reinvestment of dividends

Year end	1987	1988	1989	1990
Ordinary shares.				
Net yield, %	5.0	4.5	5.0	4.0
Number	200	209	219	228
Price/share	50	55	65	60
Value, £	**100.0**	**115.0**	**142.6**	**136.9**
All Share Index.				
Target yield, %	4.2	4.6	4.2	4.9
Target number	200	209	218	229
Targ price/share	50.0	52.0	67.6	58.3
Target value, £	**100.0**	**108.7**	**147.4**	**133.2**
RPI	103.3	110.6	119.1	130.1
AlShI	891	926	1205	1038.4

Definitions:

a) It is assumed that there is one dividend per year, paid at the end of each year.

b) The number of shares increases, as the net dividends are reinvested to buy more shares. The equation is:

$$\text{Number}\,(x+1) = \text{Number}\,(x) \times (1 + \text{NetYield}/100)$$

c) $\text{Targ price}(x+1) = \text{Targ price}(x) \times \text{AlShI}(x+1)/\text{AlShI}(x)$

that there is only one dividend paid each year and it is paid at the end of the year. This assumption can result in a significant error, since the share price on the day the dividend is paid could be quite different to the price at the end of the year.

The conclusion is that monitoring the value of £100 invested in each individual share in an investor's portfolio is not a method suitable for inclusion in the System, but that inspection of this information, as found in the financial magazines, etc., can be of assistance in deciding which shares to buy.

APPENDIX 6

Alternative methods for monitoring portfolio performance

AVERAGE OF THE P/A RATIO OF INDIVIDUAL SHARES

The use of the *P/A ratio* to monitor the performance of individual shares is part of the System and was described in Chapter 5. The performance of a portfolio of shares could be calculated by averaging the *P/A ratio* of all the shares in the portfolio. The average could be calculated on each of a series of dates and the trend of this figure with time could be monitored and compared with changes in the Retail Price Index. The average of the ratios could be calculated for each category of share in the portfolio so that the relative performance of the categories could be compared. The entry in the 1985 column for UT 'E' is seen to be 1.20p; this figure is ignored when the averages are calculated. It will be remembered that the letter p indicates that it is

Table A6.1 Average of the P/A ratio of shares

| | P/A ratio | | | | |
	1984	1985	1986	1987	1988
Ord.shares					
A	0.80	0.90	0.95	0.95	1.00
B	1.15	1.15	1.15	1.10	1.00
Average(OrdSh)	0.98	1.03	1.05	1.03	1.00
Unit Trusts					
C	1.00	0.95	1.00	1.15	1.00
D	0.90	1.00	1.05	1.05	1.00
E		1.20p	1.10	0.95	1.00
Average(UT)	0.95	0.98	1.05	1.05	1.00
Average(Total)	0.96	1.00	1.05	1.04	1.00

derived from the purchase price of the holding of 'E' units and that the units were purchased partway through the review period (see Chapter 5).

The figures in the example in Table A6.1 show that the *P/A ratios* of the ordinary shares have increased by 2 per cent (0.98 – 1.00) over the five years, whereas the unit trusts have gained 5 per cent. The performance of the whole portfolio has grown by 4 per cent. The ordinary shares, the unit trusts and, indeed, the whole portfolio have therefore beaten the All Share Index.

It is seen that the average of the *P/A ratios* provides useful information, in that it indicates whether the choice of investments has been above or below average. A comparison of the movement of the average of the *P/A ratios* with the Retail Price Index can also give an indication of the effectiveness of the timing of the purchases/sales. For the reasons outlined in Chapter 6, however, the use of the average *real return* is preferred as a means of assessing the average performance of the shares selected to form the portfolio.

AVERAGE OF THE REAL GROWTH/RETURN OF INDIVIDUAL SHARES

Investors not only want to know the performance of their portfolio, but also the reasons for the level of performance achieved. The average of the *real growth* and the yield, or alternatively the *real return*, of the individual shares can provide useful information on one aspect of portfolio performance, in that it indicates whether the choice of investments has been above or below average. This method has been described in Chapter 11. By comparing the average of the *real returns* of the individual shares with the *real return* calculated for the whole portfolio, additional information can be obtained. The reasons for the differences can be analysed under four headings:

Share choice: This refers to the choice of shares for inclusion in the portfolio. Choice is being made, of course, not only on purchase but also when deciding whether to hold or sell a holding. If the performance of the shares is, according to the average, falling behind the *target*, then the choice is poor.

Weight: This refers to the relative size of each of the holdings. If the size of the holdings in the better performing shares is lower than in the poorer performing shares, the portfolio performance will be lower than the average and the weighting is poor.

Buy/sell timing: This refers to the timing of any aquisitions or disposals. The timing is poor if a shareholding is purchased when the market is at its peak, i.e. if, after purchase, for instance, the All Share Index starts to fall and the Retail Price Index to rise. This will result in low *real* and *target growths*, as measured by both methods.

Purchase/sale costs: As the activity of the portfolio, in terms of the buying and selling of shares, increases, so the performance of the portfolio as a whole will fall behind the average of the individual shares, other things being equal. Other things should not, of course, be equal, since the purpose of the increased activity is to replace poorly performing shares with better performing shares.

These examples give only a limited view of the possible permutations in explaining the reasons for the level of performance achieved by a portfolio. They are sufficient, however, to indicate that the extra information provided by the average performance can be useful, whilst confirming that a significant degree of judgement is needed when interpreting the meaning of the figures.

PEPS

The System outlined in Chapter 5 for monitoring share prices is applicable to most Peps (Personal Equity Plans), providing there has been no further investment in the Pep after the initial investment. This is so, despite the fact that Peps do not express their value in terms of share or unit prices, but only in terms of the £ value of the investment. The calculations used for single shares in Chapter 5 can be used for Peps by treating the Pep as one share, so that the value of the Pep is substituted for the price of the share in the equations. An obvious method of analysis, analogous to the use of the *P/A ratio* for individual shares, is to monitor the ratio of the £ value of the Pep to the AlShI ; better still is to calculate the *real return* of the Pep (see example in Table A6.2 below):

Table A6.2 Ratio of Pep value to AlShI, and real return

Year end	1987	1988	1989	1990
Pep value,£	500	530	740	650
Pep val/AlShI	0.56	0.57	0.61	0.63
Pep val/AlShI(re-b'd)	**0.90**	**0.91**	**0.98**	**1.00**
Period to end 1990				
% Inflation/a	8.0	8.5	9.2	
% Pep growth/a	9.1	10.7	−12.2	
% AlShI growth/a	5.2	5.9	−13.9	
% Real return/a	**1**	**2**	**−24**	
% Targ return/a	**−3**	**−3**	**−25**	
AlShI	891	926	1205	1038
RPI	103.3	110.6	119.1	130.1

Definitions:

a)   The definitions of the intermediate variables and the *target return/a* can be found in Chapter 5.

b)   Since the dividends are reinvested:
    % Real return/a = % Real growth/a
             = % (Pep growth − Infl)/(1 + Infl/100)

Looking first of all at the figures for the RPI, AlShI, Pep value and rebased ratio, Pep val/AlShI, the Pep analysed in Table A6.2 has increased in value by 30 per cent, over the period 1987 to 1990, but because the RPI has increased by 26 per cent, the value of the Pep has, in fact, only risen by about 4 per cent in real terms, i.e. approximately 1 per cent per annum. The ratio 'Pep value/AlShI' has increased by 11 per cent over the review period, indicating that the Pep has outperformed the All Share Index. It must be remembered, of course, that in most Peps the dividends are reinvested, so the rate of growth of the investment value would be expected to be greater than for normal shares, and greater than the All Share Index.

The performance of the Pep is more suitably monitored by calculating the *%real return* and comparing it with the *target return*, because this method is better for investments in which the dividends are reinvested. It is seen that the *real return* has been significantly better than the *target return*, particularly over the longer term. The methods outlined here for Peps are simple and easy to use, but a more rigorous analysis can be achieved by treating the Pep as if it were a portfolio using the methods explained in Chapter 6. This approach has been chosen for inclusion in the System because it can accomodate injections or withdrawals of money, in contrast to the methods reviewed in the example in Table A6.2. It is demonstrated in Chapter 7 for a Save and Prosper Pep.

REPORTING PERFORMANCE AS % OF TARGET

An alternative method of reporting the performance of a share or a portfolio, is to express the chosen criteria as a percentage of the appropriate target, instead of quoting the target figure itself. For example, the way in which *real returns* are reported in the System is as follows:

> Real return = 8 % p.a., target return = 10 % p.a.
> The alternative would be:
> Real return = 8 % p.a., i.e. 80 % of target.

Some investors may well prefer this alternative. The advantage is that comparisons with target are made in a common language, e.g.

> Real return = 8 % p.a., i.e. 80 % of target.
> Real growth = 4 % p.a., i.e. 70 % of target.

The disadvantage is that investors will not see reported the value of the target.

GLOSSARY

AlShI   Financial Times Actuaries All Share Index

Categories of investment   Shares are divided into three categories, ordinary, investment trust and unit trust (including unit trust (accumulative)). Equities comprise shares and Peps. Investments comprise equities and fixed interest investment.

CGT (Capital Gains Tax)   A *real gain* is made when a share is sold at a higher price than the purchase price, after taking the effect of inflation into account. If the *real gain*,£, achieved on the sale of a number of shares, after deduction of expenses, is greater than the exemption limit, tax has to be paid on the balance.

Charting   The use of share price charts to predict future price movements. The charts present the movement of the share price, over a range of dates, in graphical form.

Companies   Companies are deemed to include those bodies issuing unit trusts, investment trusts and Peps, as well as stocks and shares.

CorPri, Pr(c) (Corrected Price)   The *corrected price* is the share price, adjusted for scrip issues, so that the trend of the *corrected price* is meaningful. The trend in the share price is not meaningful if a scrip issue has taken place.

Cover   The ratio 'Earnings per share / Net dividend per share'.

Currency format   By using the computer currency format, the number in a cell is highlighted but can still be used in equations, functions, etc. In the System the letter 'p' is used to indicate that the contents of the cell are not related to the date at the top of the column, but are related to the purchase or sale price.

DCF (Discounted Cash Flow)   The DCF method for measuring the rate of return on an investment is commonly used by industry and commerce.

End date   The date at or near the end of the review period, which together with the start date, defines the period over which the performance criteria are being measured. The calculation of growth rates, for instance, are normally carried out over the period from the start date to the end date.

Equities   The category comprising ordinary shares, unit trusts, investment trusts and Peps.

Exemption limit   Tax is paid on *real gains*, less expenses, which exceed the exemption limit.

FIInv (Fixed Interest Investment)   The category comprising preference shares, loan stock, gilt-edged stocks, and bank and building society savings accounts.

Floppy disk   A disk on which a computer can store information, or from which it can read information. The disk supplied with this book contains general market information and the performance data for the Selected Portfolio. (Tables 13.1, 13.2, 13.3 and 13.4).

Functions   Built-in functions in computer spreadsheets which avoid the need for users to write their own formulae. The Lotus functions used in the book are listed together with the Excel equivalent:

	Lotus	*Excel*
Average of a range of numbers	@AVG	=AVERAGE
Serial number of a date	@DATE	=DATE
Internal rate of return of a range of cash flows	@IRR	=IRR
Interest rate per period	@RATE	=RATE
Sum of figures in a range	@SUM	=SUM

Fundamental analysis   The analysis of the information in company reports, particularly the profit and loss account, the balance sheet and the cash flow statement, with a view to forecasting future performance.

Growth rate   The rate of growth in the price of the share, or the value of the portfolio.

The rate of growth is determined for a share by the @RATE function.

The rate of growth is determined for a portfolio over a period of years, by the direct (T&E) method, involving a trial and error calculation. It can be determined indirectly (IRR method) by calculating the % Return (IRR) and then using the equation:

$$\% \text{ Growth/a.} = \% \text{ Return/a.} - \% \text{ Net Yield}$$

Infl   Per cent inflation per annum

Infl Price P(i) or Price(i) (Inflated Price)   The *inflated price* is calculated by taking the Share Price on the start date, and scaling it up by the RPI.

Inside information   Unpublished information about a company's recent performance and prospects, known to only a few investors, who can make a profit at the expense of other investors, by buying or selling shares.

Inter-bank rate   The three month inter-bank rate of interest, a guide to interest rates in general for fixed interest investments.

Intermediate variables   These are variables that are calculated as an intermediate step towards the determination of the performance criteria. They include the *corrected price*, inflation rate, *inflated price*, price growth and portfolio value growth. The All Share Index growth rate is an intermediate variable in the steps towards the calculation of the *target growth*.

Inv (Invested)   Amount invested in portfolio in each interval, e.g. year or quarter. Purchases are positive and sales negative.

InvFrac (Invested fraction)

$InvFrac = \text{Inv} \times \text{Days} / 365$

where Days = days between date of purchase or sale and end of year.

IRR (Internal rate of return) The internal rate of return of a portfolio, measured using the @IRR(Guess Number, Range of Cash Flows) function in the Lotus spreadsheet program.

Labels Computer terminology for headings, along the horizontal and vertical axes of a table.

Market statistics The market statistics recorded in Table 13.1 provide the information needed to understand the performance of investments in general. The performance of the different indices since 31 March 1982 are reviewed, together with the three-month inter-bank rate.

Msp Measuring share performance.

MspData *MspData* is the name of the computer file containing information about the stocks and shares held, and the investments made. (Table 13.2 for the *selected portfolio*).

MspFIInv *MspFIInv* is the name of the computer file containing the performance criteria for the fixed interest investments.

MspPri *MspPri* is the name of the computer file containing the performance criteria for the individual shares. (Table 13.3 for the *selected portfolio*).

MspPort *MspPort* is the name of the computer file containing the performance criteria of the portfolio. (Table 13.4 for the *selected portfolio*).

No.& Scrip (Number and Scrip) The number of shares owned on 31 March 1982, plus shares received in any subsequent scrip (including capitalisation or bonus) issue.

If no shares were owned on 31 March 1982, then No. & scrp is equal to the number purchased in the first lot or tranche since that date, plus any subsequent scrip issues. This figure does not include any shares purchased after the first lot, whether as a straightforward purchase of an extra lot with new money, or by reinvesting the dividend, or by taking up a rights issue. Nor does the figure include scrip issue shares related to shares purchased after the first lot.

Ord Ordinary shares.

P/A ratio (Price(c)/AlShI ratio, rebased) The ratio 'Corrected price / All Share Index' i.e. 'Price(c) / AlShI', rebased to 1.0 on a chosen date.

P/E ratio (Price/Earnings ratio) The ratio 'Price per share/Net earnings per share'.

Pep (Personal equity plans) Equity investments for which the dividends and capital gains are tax free.

Performance criteria The criteria calculated as part of the System, to measure the performance of a share or portfolio, e.g. *P/A ratio, real gain, real growth* and *real return*. Other performance criteria are abstracted from the financial press, e.g. yield and P/E ratios.

Portfolio   Holdings of shares in a number of different companies.

Pr/sh (Price per share)   The following prices are used:
Ordinary and investment trust shares – middle price.
Unit trusts – bid price.

Real growth, %Real gr/a (Per cent real growth per annum)   The *real growth* is determined from the %Growth/a by using the equation:

$$Real\ growth = (\%\,Growth - Infl) / (1 + Infl/100)$$

Real return, %Real ret/a (Per cent real return per annum)   Approximate relationship:

$$Real\ return\ (T\&E) = \%\,Real\ growth/a(T\&E) + \%\,Yield(net).$$

Direct calculation for a portfolio:
Real return (IRR) = Internal rate of return of a range of cash flows, using the Lotus @IRR function.

Rebasing   A range of figures can be rebased by dividing each one by the rebasing constant. The objective is to make it easier to compare the pattern of change in a number of ranges, by ensuring that they all have the same rebased value on a predetermined date.

RGain (Real gain)

$$Real\ gain = Corrected\ price - Inflated\ price$$

RPI (Retail Price Index)   Changes in the RPI are a measure of the rate of inflation.

Review period   The period of time over which the performance criteria are measured.

Rights issue   An issue of new shares in a company, offered to existing shareholders in proportion to their present holding, at a predetermined price.

Scrip issue   An issue of new shares in a company, offered to existing shareholders in the company in proportion to their present holding, at no cost to the shareholder.

Selected Portfolio   A portfolio of shares chosen to demonstrate the application of the System of performance measurement. The performances of the shares in the *selected portfolio*, and the portfolio as a whole are shown in Tables 13.3 and 13.4.

Shares (Sh)   The category comprising ordinary shares, unit trusts and investment trusts. Shares are in the Equity category, together with Peps.

Share Transfer   Transfer of ownership of shares.

Start Date   The date on which the period of the performance review starts.

Stocks   Fixed interest investments (including preference shares, although these are more correctly termed shares or equity).

System   The system of investment performance measurement recommended in this book, for use by the private investor.

Takeover   The purchase of one company by another company, the share-holders of the bid-for company being offered cash or shares in the bidding company, or a mixture of both.

Target   A standard against which the performance criteria can be judged. The target is the value of the performance criteria when it is assumed that the share(s) has tracked the All Share Index.

Target growth, %Targ gr/a (Per cent target growth per annum)   The *target growth* is the rate of growth in the price of the share, or the value of the portfolio, after allowing for inflation, with the assumption that the share price(s) tracks the All Share Index

Target return, %Targ ret/a (Per cent target return per annum)   The *target return* is the sum of the *target growth* and the *target yield* (net).

Target yield, %Targ yield (Per cent target yield)   The *target yield* is the yield of the shares making up the All Share Index (AlShI). The gross yield is quoted in the *Financial Times* and other publications.

Tax Voucher   See Warrants.

T&E (Trial and error)   The name of the direct method used in the System to measure the growth rate of a portfolio over a period of years.

UT   Unit trusts.

UT(Acc) (Unit trust (accumulative))   Unit trust units whose number remains constant but whose value/unit increases as a result of reinvesting the dividends, net of basic rate tax.

Value copied   The normal computer copying facility will copy the content of a cell, even if it is a formula, to another cell. When it is desired to copy only the value calculated by the formula, and not the formula itself, this is called value copying.

Warrants   Also called tax vouchers. These are the forms attached to the dividend cheque, which record the net dividend in pence per share and in £ value, and the tax credit. The number of shares held is normally quoted.
   Warrant is also a term used in relation to options, but this is not a subject considered in this book.

Yield   The % Yield on a particular date is equal to the dividend(s) per share received over the past year, divided by the share price on that date. The gross yield is calculated on the dividend before deduction of basic rate tax, whilst the net yield is calculated after deduction of tax.

INDEX